SPIES

Books compiled by Richard Davis

SPIES
The True Story

RICHARD DAVIS

HUTCHINSON
London Melbourne Sydney Auckland Johannesburg

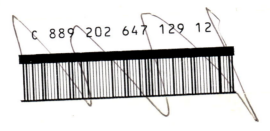

Hutchinson Junior Books Ltd

An imprint of the Hutchinson Publishing Group
17–21 Conway Street, London W1P 6JD

Hutchinson Group (Australia) Pty Ltd
30-32 Cremorne Street, Richmond South, Victoria 3121
PO Box 151, Broadway, New South Wales 2007

Hutchinson Group (NZ) Ltd
32-34 View Road, PO Box 40-086, Glenfield, Auckland 10

Hutchinson Group (SA) (Pty) Ltd
PO Box 337, Bergvlei 2012, South Africa

First published 1982
© Richard Davis 1982

Set in Plantin by Fleet Graphics, Enfield, Middlesex

Printed in Great Britain by The Anchor Press Ltd
and bound by Wm Brendon & Son Ltd,
both of Tiptree, Essex

Davis, Richard
  Spies.
  1. Espionage – History – Juvenile literature
  I. Title
  327.1′2′09   UB270.5

ISBN 0 09 149420 6

For Trish

ACKNOWLEDGEMENTS

My grateful thanks to the BBC for allowing me to include information on the codebusting operation at Bletchley Park from the Radio 4 copyrighted series 'The Profession of Intelligence' by Dr Christopher Andrew; and to Sidgwick and Jackson for permission to quote from *John Vassall: Autobiography of a Spy* (1975).

I have consulted many other books, too numerous to mention here, but I would like to thank the Library Staff of Blandford Forum Public Library for their tireless help in getting through material with the minimum delay.

R.D

Contents

1
What Is Espionage?

I was once placed under surveillance by the secret police of an Iron Curtain country.

Believe me, when I discovered what was going on, and had been going on for at least a week, I felt pretty spooked.

They were very discreet about it, those watchers. I had been allowed to travel around sightseeing, without any apparent check being placed on my movements. At the beginning of my stay in this particular country, I had been allocated an official interpreter and guide by the government, plus an official spending allowance which was more than generous, and I had been told that whenever I was not working my time would be my own. I was, officially, allowed to go anywhere. But with the wisdom of hindsight I now realize that if I had shown myself too interested, too curious about certain aspects of that country's life and society, I might have been escorted somewhere, very politely but firmly, for questioning.

You see, I wasn't just an English tourist on holiday.

At that time, in 1968, I was involved very much in communications. I was working for the B B C and I was also writing regular articles and columns for a magazine. So I was a journalist. And Iron Curtain countries are wary of journalists from the West.

The magazine I was writing for had asked me to go and cover a film festival in Hungary. I was the only British journalist in the party; of course I jumped at the chance to visit Hungary, see a lot of films, particularly ones that wouldn't necessarily be shown over here, and interview some top Hungarian actors and directors, as well as actually getting paid for doing so!

The festival itself is a regular yearly event, and is held at Pecs, a very attractive little town in the hills near the Austrian border. I was taken to meet the local Communist Party secretary, who was extremely affable and drove me in his personal car to and from several parties, and even tried to arrange a special performance of the Hungarian State Ballet for me to attend. I was wined and dined and saw some excellent films. I was even asked if I would like to spend my holidays there, and also to write on a regular basis about the British film industry (we had one then!) for a Hungarian film annual. And so on.

But I was being watched all the time, and my movements duly noted.

This is how I found out. When the festival was over I had been asked by Hungarofilm, the state-owned Hungarian film company, to spend a few days in Budapest, the Hungarian capital, as their guest. They would take me round some studios, show me some more films and I would be free to do some sightseeing on my own. My interpreter, a student studying English at the university, would translate the films for me as my Hungarian leaves something to be desired!

On the last night of my stay I had been invited to a

farewell party. All the other journalists had gone home and I was on my own for a few days. I didn't get back to my hotel till very late and as I had to catch a plane back to London very early the next morning, I decided that it simply wasn't worth going to bed at all. I would pack my suitcase very quietly so as not to disturb the people in the nearby rooms, lie down on the bed fully clothed to get a couple of hours' sleep, have a wash and then go downstairs to wait for the dining room to open for an early breakfast. Then the car was due to arrive at the hotel to take me to the airport. I had of course taken extensive notes of the films I had seen and the impressions of the Hungarian film industry that I had formed, but I had decided not to write the finished article till I got back to England and could collate my thoughts at my leisure.

I lay down on the bed but was afraid to go to sleep in case I didn't wake up in time and wasn't ready for the taxi when it arrived. So instead I decided to go downstairs a good deal earlier than had been my original plan.

The door of my bedroom, on the third floor, was immediately opposite the lift. As I opened that door – very quietly because it was still only about 3.30 in the morning – I heard a lift start up. It had obviously been on another floor; now it slid quietly to rest in front of me, the lift door opened, an attendant stepped out, practically grabbed my arm and said, 'Can I help you, sir?'

I hadn't even rung for the lift, I had certainly made no sound to rouse the man from another floor, and in any case I was surprised that an attendant should be on duty all night. When I told him my reasons for leaving my room so early, I was politely but firmly escorted to the ground floor and shown where to wait.

After this I realized that in all probability I had been watched since arriving in Budapest, possibly even before the festival in Pecs, and that my hotel room had equally probably been bugged and searched as a matter of course. Not because they suspected me of anything, but purely because it was routine procedure.

Little things that had struck me as odd during my time in Hungary now assumed greater significance. For example, my interpreter had asked me if I would meet some of the friends from his class in college to talk about life in England. I had agreed, we had arranged to meet at a café one evening – in fact I had cut short a previous appointment to be prompt – and then nobody had turned up! Had they been warned off? Sometimes the authorities don't like young people to learn too much about life in the West. My young friend himself told me he was totally baffled, but refused to talk much about it when I saw him the next day. Things like that happen all the time; you have to accept it and not think too much about it afterwards.

But every time I think about the incident of the lift attendant stepping silently out of the shadows in a deserted hotel corridor, unsummoned, at 3.30 in the morning, I still feel the back of my neck prickling!

It was like something out of a James Bond novel, happening for real. And 3.30 is the hour that the secret police like to knock on your door because it is the time when the metabolism of the human body is at its very slowest.

So I had to revise my feelings about the subject of espionage. You see, when you set out to write a book about real-life spies, you say to yourself, I want to show my readers that in reality espionage is *not* like a James Bond novel. Real spies are little grey men, unobtrusively melting into the background, only too anxious to avoid the limelight. *Real* espionage is an unglamorous business, full of boring, day-to-day undramatic routine. Well, to a great extent that, of course, is true. It is only the unsuccessful spies that we can write about, because it is only the unsuccessful spies that are caught. The successful spies are still operating, and the old truism that there are bigger fish in the sea than ever came out of it is only too sinisterly accurate in this context.

But –

The more you research, the more you are confronted by the inescapable fact that a great many aspects of the espionage game are *exactly* like a James Bond tale!

For instance, take the case of the limpet microphones and the embassy buggings. We all know that real-life bugging goes on all the time, particularly in embassies, and limpets have been widely used since the mid-fifties. If you attach one to the outside of a building you can pick up every sound inside the nearest room. The limpet mike most commonly used is smaller than a matchbox and agents can sit in a car or a hotel room up to five miles away and, using a tape recorder, receive messages sent by ultra-shortwave radio. Agents can then reduce the tape recording to microdot size.

The first officially acknowledged discovery of a limpet mike was made outside the Iranian embassy in Moscow. Probably a window-cleaner had attached it to the window of the ambassador's first-floor office. A rash of the mikes were discovered between 1956 and 1965 on the outsides of buildings belonging to the Allies in West Berlin and on offices of various other centres of the German Federal Republic, including those in Paris, Brussels, London, Washington and Rome.

The embassies of other countries in Moscow were continually finding electronic listening devices, as they're called, while, tit for tat, Russia herself, and other satellite countries, found similar ones: in the Soviet secret service headquarters, the foreign ministry and other administrative buildings, not only in Moscow itself but also in Budapest, Leipzig, Prague and Warsaw.

In the spring of 1964, security officers attached to the United States embassy in Moscow knew that there was a serious security leak coming from somewhere inside the embassy. Employees were questioned and cleared and a thorough search of all the rooms got nowhere. By chance one of the security staff remembered that the building which housed the embassy had originally been three storeys lower. Before the embassy had moved there from previous premises, Soviet workmen had added the extra storeys to the seven-storey building because extra space was wanted. A further search was made on the outside of the building, and plaster and brickwork were peeled away. American faces were said to turn red! The third interior walls of the three top storeys contained wires connecting up forty different microphones! Each microphone was attached to a wooden peg that went right through the walls almost to the surface of the plaster. So, for over ten years, hundreds of conferences held in the United States embassy had been transmitted word-for-word to Soviet intelligence headquarters. Bond couldn't have capped *that* one!

The Americans don't always learn their lesson. They should have profited by the experience of what happened as early as 1945, when Soviet diplomats in Moscow presented Mr Averell Harriman, at that time United States ambassador to Russia, with a carved replica of the United States

Great Seal. Mr Harriman was touched by this Russian gesture of good will. Proudly he placed the present in an honoured position in the ambassadorial study in the embassy. It wasn't until 1952 that security men discovered that the shield was an ingenious spying device. It was made of wood and inside it was a hollowed-out cavity. Inside the cavity was a U-shaped piece of metal with a steel-spring vibrator attached. The vibrator reacted to the soundwaves of conversations held in Mr Harriman's study; directly across the street from the embassy, Soviet intelligence agents had installed a radar device, highly sensitive and focused on the vibrator. Its reactions were then registered on the radar scanner and converted back into sound. So for seven years every conversation held in Mr Harriman's private study had been monitored to the Russians.

These are just two of the more sensational examples of listening devices detected at top level. The gadgetry employed in the history of espionage would need a complete library to itself.

When we come to discuss the celebrated Portland spy ring, we'll learn of some of the equipment found in a certain bungalow in the London suburb of Ruislip.

In espionage, small is beautiful. American scientists have manufactured a radio transmitter no larger than a lump of sugar. It uses up to five transistors which can draw power from an ordinary car battery or a telephone system.

Mr Kroger, the owner of that Ruislip bungalow, used microdots for sending his information to Moscow. In microcopy, the dot on the *i* in the word 'microdots' could itself conceal a page of print equivalent to the page you are reading now. Think about that and its implications.

In writing a book of this size about espionage, we can only scratch the surface, the very tip of the iceberg. As the old music-hall joke has it, and quite rightly, there are indeed spies everywhere. And spies that spy, not only on ostensibly hostile forces, but on their friendly allies as well. British spies tell us things we want to know about America, as well as about Russia.

When we consider the Second World War, for example, we see that loyalties can get very blurred indeed. Atom spies like Klaus Fuchs, Alan Nunn May; spies in the Foreign Office like Guy Burgess, Donald Maclean, Kim Philby, Anthony Blunt or George Blake, were all supplying secret information to Russia, information that America and Britain would have preferred her not to have, despite the fact that she was officially on our side till the defeat of Germany in 1945. After that, when the Cold War started, and Russia became our opponent, they went on spying. Who was, or was not, Britain's ally at any given moment was of little consequence to them, as their loyalties were, first and last, to the Soviet Union. Looking back over the Second World War, it's sometimes hard to remember that Russia *was* our ally. The fact that Nunn May, as he declared in his defence after he had been arrested, couldn't see why Russia shouldn't have our atomic secrets because we were all on the same side, didn't cut any ice with the prosecution and didn't stop him from getting a prison sentence.

Right from the time when the Soviets first established a communist state in Russia, after the Bolshevik revolution and the overthrow of the Tsar in 1917, as far as the British secret service was concerned Soviet Russia was always the bogeyman. Churchill always hated the Communists, and when circumstances decreed that he had to ally himself with Stalin in order to defeat Nazi Germany, he never overcame his uneasiness and distrust. When Germany and Japan surrendered in 1945, he was the first to warn the West about the 'iron curtain' that had descended across Eastern Europe. In fact he invented the title. So, right through the war years, official policy dictated that the Russians should be told just as much as it was necessary for them to know, and no more. With America, in contrast, information was pooled far more generously.

History has taught that countries can be friends one minute, enemies the next. Britain fought a bitter war against America when America wanted to break away from the domination of the mother country. At that time we executed American spies and America eliminated ours. When Napoleon came to power, France was our greatest enemy. And so the cycle goes.

Consequently the uncomfortable truth must be that every country has spies sending back information about every other country, peaceful, hostile – or neutral.

In that American War of Independence, George Washington wrote in a letter to Colonel Elias Dayton on 26 July 1777:

The necessity of procuring good Intelligence is apparent and need not be further urged. All that remains for me to add is that you keep the whole matter as secret as possible. For upon Secrecy, Success depends in most Enterprises of the kind, and for want of it, they are generally defeated, however well planned and promising a favourable issue.

That dictum is as true today as when he wrote it.

In this book we'll talk about some of the most celebrated

cases and some of the most colourful personalities. But we must never forget that the ultimate spy story can never be written, because the successful spy never gets caught.

First, we should look at some of the terminology of espionage. What are dead-letter drops? What is a cutout?

As a matter of fact most of the terms current in espionage jargon were originally invented by mystery writers, some of whom went to work for real-life intelligence, as we shall see. Fact just copied fiction.

Dead-letter drops are places where reports can be left and picked up by someone else. Many spies work on the theory that the more obvious the place, the less carefully will it be searched. Public libraries, cinemas, the benches in public parks, even spaces between the struts of a bridge, all these places have been used.

Perhaps the most uncommon hiding place of all, and one that strictly speaking isn't a 'place' at all, was chosen by a lady spy who was recruited by British intelligence in 1963 and who operated in Moscow.

Most women visit hairdressing salons and it's not exactly a suspicious event to do so, even in Soviet Russia. So this master spy (who was also a spymaster because she had agents working for her) left orders that whenever any of her agents visited the salon, the hairdresser was to remove from their carefully arranged curls the microfilm they had hidden there. Later, when the spymaster visited the salon, the hairdresser was to dress into her hair the same miniature containers . . . .

A spy was arrested in France while working for East Germany. He had taken a job in a French aviation plant. The police found in his pocket a bag of fruit drops. The sweets were cut open and inside each one were tiny pieces of microfilm revealing top-secret information on the new French Concorde.

Public lavatories are favourite places for leaving packets to be picked up later. There's the oft-repeated story of an agent who used the cistern tank in a certain cubicle in a London underground station lavatory for leaving his microfilm. But when his contact came to collect it on one occasion he found the cubicle closed for plumbing repairs. Closed and locked. The cubicle remained out of order for a fortnight and at the end of that time when the contact was finally able to get inside, he found the microfilm still concealed, safe and sound. A similar story is told by Greville Wynne in a later chapter of this book. John Vassall, the Admiralty spy, nearly lost his papers altogether in the gents' loo at Drury Lane Theatre! More about that too, later.

There is a phrase that is often used in intelligence circles, and that is 'need to know'. We've seen that it applied collectively to Soviet Russia during the Second World War and Russia obviously felt the same about us. A spy is usually kept in as much ignorance as possible about the wider implications of the information he is paid to get. He passes it to a cutout, who in his turn takes it on to the next stretch of its journey until it reaches its final destination.

When you stop to think about it, the reasons for this are obvious. A spy is told only what he needs to know because he may be captured and interrogated, and the less he knows about the overall operation, the less he can give others away. As we will see, over and over again, spies are initially caught not because of incriminating evidence, but because they are betrayed and their names given by defectors – those who run away from their own countries to seek refuge elsewhere.

Today a spy usually operates as part of a network, a group of agents controlled by a spymaster. Gordon Lonsdale and Colonel Rudolph Abel were spymasters, controlling a ring of agents answerable to them. (They were also master spies, but that isn't necessarily the same thing!) The days of the daring and dashing freelances, the Jules Silbers and the Eddie Chapmans, are long gone.

So the 'need to know' principle is what governs intelligence departments generally. Nobody except the head of the department knows everything about an operation – and sometimes not even *he* does!

There are an awful lot of initials in modern espionage. So in order not to get hopelessly confused, we should look at a few of the organizations that control it.

So what exactly are the KGB, the CIA, the OSS? What is the difference between MI5 and MI6?

Boiled down to its most simple form, we can say that in Britain the active organization of espionage is the business of MI6, sometimes referred to as the SIS, the Special Intelligence Service; counter-espionage, the detection and tracking down of spies, is the responsibility of MI5, which works very closely with the Special Branch of Scotland Yard.

In America, the FBI, the Federal Bureau of Investigation, sometimes known as the Company, catches spies, and it is the CIA, the Central Intelligence Agency, that uses them. But when the Watergate scandal set all America by its ears and led to the resignation of President Nixon, it became pretty obvious that the CIA does – or did – other things as well.

Rumours flew around that the CIA had tried to influence

the foreign policy of other countries, though no definite proof was ever published officially. People got very hot under the collar about attempted political assassinations, but again no proof was ever published. It is no bad thing when an organization in danger of getting too big for its boots is openly investigated, and the CIA was subjected to the spotlight of very concentrated public scrutiny after Watergate.

Intelligence in any country can't afford plaster sainthood. Espionage is a dirty business, and dirty tricks can't be avoided. It would be as unrealistic to believe that they could as to assume that intelligence services, anywhere, could be made up solely of double-dyed villains.

The CIA drew and developed out of the OSS, the Office of Strategic Services, which used to parachute agents into enemy-occupied countries during the Second World War, usually to liaise with the Resistance, the underground army of loyal freedom fighters. In Britain, the SOE, the Special Operations Executive, did the same. In the early days of the CIA, a lot of its agents came to Britain to study the methods and procedure of our secret service; just as Westminster is called the Mother of Parliaments because our parliamentary procedure is taken as the model for the constitutions of many other countries, the same situation applies to our secret services.

In Russia, espionage is organized into two categories: military and civil (or civilian). The GRU looks after the military and the KGB the civil. It is the KGB, the dreaded secret police, whom Western spies must watch. The secret service HQ is known as the Moscow Centre, situated in the Lublanka Prison, where spies have so often been questioned, tortured and incarcerated. The organization

SMERSH, about which Ian Fleming wrote in the early Bond books, really does exist, its initials standing for the Russian equivalent of 'death to spies'. The speciality of the Lublanka Prison is terror.

The KGB can be ruthless and merciless if it catches Russian defectors. Escapers to the West may be considered dangerous to the state because they may be in possession of valuable knowledge. Defectors usually have to live in secret and under false names. If they themselves were members of the KGB their situation is even more perilous. Igor Gouzenko was an example of a defector whose information was so important to the West that even to this day it hasn't all been published. We'll meet him again later.

An example of KGB vengeance hit the headlines in 1979 when the unfortunate Bulgarian Georgi Markov was injected with a tiny poisoned capsule through the tip of an umbrella. It happened in a busy London street in the middle of the rush hour; apparently a similar incident had occurred earlier in Paris, the victim this time being one of Markov's colleagues. The Russian general Krevitsky, who defected to the Americans in 1937, was found murdered in a seedy hotel room in New York in 1941. We'll see later that Reino Hayhanen, the spy who betrayed Colonel Abel to the Americans, was killed in a mysterious car accident.

A former Soviet ambassador was interviewed for a BBC programme about intelligence, and this is what he had to say:

'The KGB has four or five times more personnel than the CIA, generally speaking. Even in the Soviet Union itself they follow Soviet citizens about, even if they have nothing against them. They tapped my telephone, and I know that both my apartment in Moscow and my country house had been tapped constantly. It wasn't that I was under suspicion. It's just normal routine.

The KGB have the force and power to do anything. Nothing that the CIA or any other intelligence service does can compare. The KGB can kill you – it's just as simple as that. They could take me from anywhere I may hide, cut me up into little pieces, and send my body to Moscow in the diplomatic bag! No one would do anything if I just disappeared!

The diplomatic bag is just what it sounds like: a privileged route for messages and correspondence and parcels to get from an embassy to its home country without the normal delays of a public postal service.

In 1971 there was a forcible reminder of just how far the scale of Soviet intelligence infiltration had gone, when 105 so-called Russian diplomats were expelled by order of the British Government. It's by no means certain that they were all spies, but the names of all of them had been given by a Soviet defector. As a CIA official in London said, it was basically a decision by the government to get rid of 105 troublemakers and security risks or those they weren't certain about. The Soviet defector in question was a KGB officer and his evidence was backed up by the fact that a great many of those who were sent home had been followed around the country by British security agents who had seen with their own eyes how these 'diplomats' had attempted to recruit British subjects for the KGB. They were obviously in Britain under false pretences, claiming the cover of diplomatic immunity.

This points to the difference between legal and illegal spies. You might imagine that all spies are illegal, but in espionage the two words have rather more precise meanings than that.

Legal spies are those who have a legitimate right to be in

the countries in which they are operating. Being attached to
their embassy is the usual cover. Illegal spies are here under
false names and identities, pretending to be someone else.
The Soviet spy known as Gordon Lonsdale was a case in
point. As far as is known he was a Russian KGB officer
whose real name might have been Konon Molody. Illegal
spies are not accredited to embassies, therefore they have
no legitimate pretext for being here. (This only applies to
non-British subjects, of course.)

The Soviet intelligence network is many times vaster
than both the CIA and British intelligence put together. As
well as the KGB and the GRU inside Russia, it also
controls the intelligence services of its satellites. A member
of the Czech intelligence service, who defected in 1968,
said:

The Eastern European intelligence services are really extensions
of the KGB. They are in a position where they have to report in
detail to the KGB on all their cases, and they have to give up a
promising agent if the KGB demands the right to run [use] him.
They have to clear their actions with the KGB chief resident in
the field, and also with the KGB Headquarters in Moscow. This
also includes the Cuban intelligence service, and has done so
ever since 1970.

Many people believe that the spate of recent bomb outrages
in London, the work of the IRA, was given aid from
Moscow by Soviet intelligence. The journalist Chapman
Pincher, who has written several books about spies and
spying, believes that one of the IRA's unsuccessful
terrorist attempts had as its real target Sir Maurice Old-
field, the former head of MI6. What happened was that the
IRA put a bag of explosives under a table in a restaurant

situated below the flat where Sir Maurice was living. Luckily he was unhurt. Later, when an IRA hideout was found and searched, press cuttings about him were discovered.

Sir Maurice later became coordinator of security in Northern Ireland.

Every country has its own intelligence services, and some are more efficient than others.

The differences between Eastern and Western training methods for would-be spies are very pronounced, the Eastern being the more elaborate. Bernard Hutton in his book *Women Spies* has given us a remarkable account of one East European training establishment, and it reads more like James Bond than James Bond does.

He tells us that the most unique of all the Soviet spy schools was the one known as Gaczyma. It is – or it was when the book was written in 1971 – the largest in the East, as its grounds cover 42 square miles. It's divided into four sections, three of which correspond with an English-speaking country – North America, Canada, the United Kingdom; the fourth embraces Australia, New Zealand, India and South Africa.

They are all totally self-sufficient units and for ten years the embryo spy will absorb in painstaking detail every aspect of the area in which he or she has chosen to work. At the end of the course, trainees will have become so used to this alien way of life that not even torture, brainwashing or drugs will prise the truth out of them. Apparently the spy known as Gordon Lonsdale was a successful Gaczyma graduate.

At the end of the rigorous training programme – which

naturally includes the more conventional espionage instruction as well – the candidate will be subjected to a very detailed and tough examination, which includes a mock interrogation session, and we are reliably informed that the percentage of passes is not exceptionally high!

How tame our own training programme sounds after that.

According to the CIA, the less instruction a spy receives, the better. There was a time, Miles Copeland writes in *The Real Spy World*, when the great services drilled every agent in a wide range of spy techniques. But such training can often be more of a hindrance than a help. There was the case of a spy employed by Russia and working in the Pentagon, the American war centre in Washington, who was caught because his behaviour was too professional! On returning home from work he used such elaborate ruses to shake off anyone who might be shadowing him that he aroused suspicion where none existed. Had he travelled to his house in a more normal manner, he might not have been detected. Whether he was, or was not, a graduate of Gaczyma isn't known.

Agents, on the whole, tend to be reticent about their work. The last thing they want to do is attract attention to themselves. Guy Burgess, the Foreign Office diplomat, was a rare exception. He loudly proclaimed on several occasions that he was a Comintern agent (an agent for the then Communist International), but no one believed him. The idea was just too fantastic to anyone who knew him.

Sometimes officials employed on perfectly open and above-board missions try to glamorize their roles in order to appear interesting. One of these was a man called James Boone, and retired British intelligence officers who knew

Ian Fleming think that he might well have been the inspiration for Bond.

Apparently he was a Foreign Office administration officer whose real job was to examine and check supplies of goods which delegates going out on missions to the Middle East and Africa might need, but he boasted to his girlfriends that really this rather menial position was just a cover for something much more important.

He wasn't very clever and got into several scrapes in nightclubs. In Teheran he tangled with a drunk who was bothering a girl Boone was with. He used a karate chop on his unwelcome companion and unfortunately killed him. It turned out that the dead man was a well-known heroin smuggler, wanted in five countries, and this turned Mr Boone into a romantic hero. From then on he lived a kind of Walter Mitty existence, half convincing himself that his imaginary exploits were real.

Whether he convinced Ian Fleming, or whether Fleming merely used a writer's licence, perhaps the truth is that James Bond is the Walter Mitty in all of us. Perhaps the books and films loosely based on him remain so popular because we all yearn for the glamorous world he symbolizes.

But espionage is dirty. It is full of treachery and double-dealing. While at times it may appear to be glamorous, because unavoidably the glamorous world impinges on it, the other side of the coin is remorse and despair and self-hatred. The spy is forced to betray the friends and the country that trusted him, not to mention his own family. Only the very hardest of us can learn to live with that knowledge and survive.

This book describes a few of those who did live with it.

Some thrived, others paid the price. What follows is a glimpse of a world that lies all about us, a world of dark shadows and busy, hidden activity, but a world which for most of us remains thankfully remote.

2
How It Started

Espionage has probably been with us since man first found out that he could get what he wanted quickly by guile rather than force. One stone-age caveman perhaps needed information that another possessed – maybe it was the secret of fire.

The earliest recorded intelligence report was found on a clay tablet, written some 2000 years BC by a man named Bannum who commanded a desert patrol. It was addressed to his lord in Mari, beside the Euphrates, which is where it was found, and it informed Bannum's lord that the border villages which they were attacking were exchanging fire signals. Bannum didn't know what this meant, but he intended to find out what was going on. He recommended that in the meantime the guards on the city walls should be strengthened.

This seems a fairly typical sort of message and shows us that the essential nature of intelligence hasn't changed so very much. Methods of communication have got more sophisticated, that's all.

Spies pour out of the history books. Even in the Bible there are spies. The Old Testament gives us at least nine cases of espionage, but perhaps the most famous and often quoted is the story of Moses and his spies, and of Joshua and Rahab the harlot.

The Bible tells us, 'The Lord spake unto Moses, saying, Send thou men, that they may search the land of Canaan.' So you could almost say that espionage had divine sanction.

It must have been around 1480 BC. Moses had led the twelve tribes of Israel out of Egypt, in his search for the Promised Land (twelve seems a popular Biblical number: Christ had twelve apostles, or followers). They had been staying for some time in the Paran desert. Now they had reached the borders of Canaan and Moses had heard that it was rich and fertile, but he had to be sure. He asked each of the twelve tribes to send their leading warrior to him so that he might tell them of his plans.

What in fact he wanted to know about was 'the people, whether they be strong or weak, few or many – whether they dwelt in tents or strongholds'. Aware of the risks, he sent out the twelve to collect information which could just as easily have been brought back by a single scout. The inevitable result of this was that the spies couldn't agree, so Moses did nothing. Caleb and Joshua wanted to go in for an attack at once, but the rest were too timid to act.

All twelve agreed that Canaan was indeed 'a land flowing with milk and honey', but the consensus of opinion was that the inhabitants were 'giants' and the Israelites were no match for them. Only Caleb and Joshua disagreed. Moses, uncertain of what to do, consulted with the Lord, we are told. And the Lord, a jealous God, warned Moses that only Caleb and Joshua would survive to see the Promised Land in the future, because only they were unswayed by the cowardice and vacillation that had attacked the rest. The

Old Testament God is a bloodthirsty god; he is for conquest by force. Kill first, ask questions later.

Ten of the spies died of a mysterious disease, and the Children of Israel were condemned to forty years of further wandering in the wilderness (in the Bible the number forty usually means an unspecified number). So the first Biblical spies had failed in their duty, and the long trek began.

After the death of Moses, Joshua returned to try again. He came to within walking distance of Jericho and this time he only sent two men to spy out the land.

Their trip was far more productive. Getting into Jericho at night they found themselves outside the home of Rahab, a 'woman of the town' whose house was somewhere where strangers could come and go freely with no questions asked. In espionage jargon it would today be called a safe house – the type of place where secret meetings can be arranged or agents hidden for short periods. An added advantage was that it was next to the walls marking the city boundary.

But the king of Jericho had his own intelligence system and he discovered through what we would now call counter-espionage that two representatives of the Israelite army had arrived in town and were asking questions. Security police were sent to Rahab's house and they questioned her, but she was able to convince them that the two men had gone, and the police left without instituting a search.

Rahab had concealed the spies on the roof and she now let them down the front of the house, which abutted onto the city wall, by means of a cord through the window. She was able to bargain with them that in the event of an attack her family would be spared, and she arranged that her house would be identified to the soldiers by means of a scarlet thread in the window. When Joshua attacked, Rahab's family was escorted outside the city and given accommodation in tents belonging to the army. Some versions of the story say that her house was spared when the rest of Jericho was destroyed.

As everyone knows, Jericho was razed to the ground after the Israelite priests blew down the walls of the city with their trumpets. Perhaps this was an early example of the destructive force of soundwaves; or maybe the walls would have fallen down anyway. At any rate Rahab, prostitute and informer, was spared and the coded message of the scarlet thread honoured.

The Greek historian Herodotus describes in Book V of his *Persian Wars* a very neat example of one of the oldest espionage tricks of all. About 500 BC Histaeus, ruler of Miletus but under the overall control of Darius, king of Persia, decided to rebel against him and enlisted the help of Aristagoras, his brother-in-law and cousin and the man who acted as regent while Histaeus was performing his duties at Darius's court.

Here is Herodotus's own story of the amazing ruse Histaeus used to send his message undetected through Persian territory back to Miletus:

For Histaeus, when he was anxious to give Aristagoras orders to revolt, could find but one way that was safe, as the rooms were guarded, of making his wishes known; which was by taking the trustiest of his slaves, shaving all the hair from his head, and then pricking letters upon the skin, and waiting till the hair grew again. [The message couldn't have been that urgent!] This accordingly he did; and as soon as the hair was grown, he sent the man to Miletus, giving him no other message than this, 'When you come to Miletus, bid Aristagoras shave your head, and look at it.'

Now the marks on the head, as I have clearly mentioned, were a command to revolt.

This method, owing something to the ancient art of tattooing, was employed in less drastic form by the lady we met in the last chapter, who hid microfilm in her agents' hairdos.

The disguises used in the conveying of messages have been limited only by the ingenuity of the spies themselves, and the story of Histaeus and his slave may be the earliest recorded example of the use of the microdot.

Tutankhamen, the Egyptian boy king from whose tomb was rescued a fabulous fortune, was also connected, albeit indirectly, with an example of espionage that has been recorded. Among records found in the ancient Hittite capital of Chattusas was a tablet dating from around 1370 BC relating to Tutankhamen's widow: she had had the temerity to suggest that she might be provided with another husband from among the Hittites, who at that time were menacing the Egyptian frontier. A Hittite prince, Mursitis, wanted to know if the offer was genuine and sent his chamberlain to Egypt with instructions to find out if it was part of a plot or could be accepted at its face value. 'Bring me back reliable information,' he wrote.

Sadly, as in so many true stories, we're left to guess the outcome, but it's certainly proof that spying wasn't unknown in ancient Egypt. On the contrary, the Egyptians had a well-organized state apparatus and secret service. Espionage was considered a highly skilled science.

A story that reminds us of the famous wooden horse of Troy concerns one of the guides of another Egyptian, King Thutmosis III. The guide's name was Captain Thute;

aided by his subversive connections he succeeded in smuggling 200 heavily armed soldiers into the besieged city of Jaffa, concealed inside flour sacks. They were actually sewn in and, thus camouflaged as a flour shipment, they were loaded onto ships bound for Jaffa.

Homer recounts the classic tale of the Trojan horse; Greek soldiers were hidden inside a giant equine statue and actually towed into the city by those whom they would presently massacre. In an ancient epic, *The Pentaur,* we learn that King Rameses was betrayed by the guide Paker whom he trusted completely. The treacherous Paker brought two enemy soldiers to Rameses, pretending they were deserters. They gave Rameses a false description of the Syrian army positions, and the Egyptians framed their own strategy on deliberately misleading information. Consequently their battle wagons were ambushed and destroyed by the Syrians.

The ancient Greeks were very fond of using heliography to send their messages. This was a system of flashing lights, a primitive form of code. In the Second World War, aerial reconnaisance teams adopted the same principle. There's not a lot that is new about espionage, either in its methods or those who engage in it. . . .

We've mentioned already how Soviet defectors inform British and American intelligence about names of East European agents. In ancient Greece, a defector told General Leonidas about the spy Ephialtes and how he had betrayed his army's position at Thermopylae. Leonidas was thus able to send his army out of danger. The double agent, the agent who works for both sides and occasionally ends up on the wrong one, is not a new phenomenon either. Alcibiades continually shifted sides between Sparta and

Athens and made good use of the military information he gained by these tactics.

In the Middle Ages priests were often used as spies, presumably because in the popular imagination a priest is above suspicion. In ancient times the priests of Baal, hostile to their ruler Belshazzar because he wanted to reorganize and reform the priesthood in Babylon, conducted secret negotiations which allowed Cyrus of Persia to conquer Babylon when he besieged it in 539 BC.

Priests have often indulged very cleverly and successfully in espionage. The Spanish Inquisition had a very effective spy service to rout out religious heretics. In England, Cardinal Wolsey under Henry VIII and, a few years later in France, Cardinal Richelieu and his successor Cardinal Mazarin, while nominally churchmen, were far more concerned with matters of state and used very highly developed spy systems. Dumas's famous romance *The Three Musketeers* while not giving a strictly accurate picture of Richelieu, does present a reasonably realistic picture of a climate of fear and suspicion in France at that time, most of which centred round the cardinal. These clerical statesmen had legions of paid informers. In the seventeenth and eighteenth centuries it was the Jesuit missionaries in Canada who were the only people who really knew what was going on. The famous Duke of Wellington and his intelligence officer, Major Colquhoun Grant, relied very heavily on local priests for information in the areas they marched through.

Alexander of Macedon, known as Alexander the Great, invented what we call postal espionage, as well as making extensive use of codes and ciphers. How he did that was particularly ingenious: he used a simple scroll and staff.

Those in his army who sent and received letters all had identical staffs and batons. The scroll containing the message, concealed in an apparently innocent letter or report, was wound spirally round the staff in such a way that one marked character on the narrow scroll coincided with a mark on the staff. The secret message could then be read from the characters which appeared in a straight line down the staff.

As far as we know, this is the first time a coding system was used as a matter of routine, though it's probable that the Chinese first invented the code as a means of passing secret information. Anyhow, what is certain is that the whole elaborate and complex system of codes and ciphers which led in the Second World War to the Ultra decoding operation at Bletchley Park has grown up very largely as a result of Alexander's practice.

But he was an innovator in other directions as well. He invented postal censorship, something that is now an essential part of wartime espionage activity and which was used to devastating effect by Jules Silber in the First World War. Alexander's invention came about quite by chance, because there was a lot of unrest in his army and he wanted to find out who the main troublemakers were. So he got all the soldiers to write letters home and then sent couriers to intercept the mail. As a result one of his officers, Phidias, was executed for treason.

Sun Tzu, the Chinese military authority who wrote his *Art of War* in the fourth century BC, said, 'Those who know the enemy as well as they know themselves will never suffer defeat. What enables the wise sovereign and good general to strike and conquer and achieve things beyond the reach of ordinary men, is foreknowledge.' That is the essential lesson of espionage, and we're still learning it today.

In the era before Christianity there were comparatively few sovereigns and generals who recognized the value of foreknowledge. One general who did was the Roman, Scipio Africanus. Sextus Frontinus, the writer of one of the earliest military manuals, *Stratagems,* tells of a mission sent by Scipio to Numidia under the command of a civilian envoy named Cornelius Lelius. The king of Numidia had agreed to receive the envoy and discuss a peace treaty with him provided that none of Scipio's soldiers was present. What he didn't know was that the crafty Scipio had indeed sent Roman officers on the mission, but that they were disguised as slaves and servants. Lelius the envoy pitched his camp near the Numidian king, whose name was Syphax. Frontinus tells the story:

These men [the Romans in disguise], in order to examine more freely the situation of the camp, purposely let loose a horse, and chased it around the greatest part of the fortifications, pretending it was running away. [Presumably it was only half-broken.] After they had reported the results of their observations, the destruction of the army soon brought the war to a close.

While they were at the camp, a small slip almost betrayed Scipio's spies completely. One of King Syphax's officers thought he recognized someone among the bogus slaves and challenged him, 'You're not a slave, you're a general!'

Lelius resorted to a system of bluff. He turned to the 'slave', and sharply slapped his face. As Frontinus reports it, 'He spat at the man and between blows, abused him thus: "You dog, you dirty slave, how dare you presume even to resemble a Roman general!" ' Perhaps this loses in translation, but we get the message, as indeed so did the 'slave'. He fell on the floor, cringing in abject remorse, and the Numidians were totally convinced that no Roman general would submit to such treatment. The man must indeed be a slave and nothing else. The ruse was successful.

The historian Livy says that on one occasion Scipio and his great opponent the Carthaginian general Hannibal – famous for taking his elephants over the Alps – met each other 'within a javelin's throw'. Livy marvels that two such generals 'fighting more bitterly against one another than any in previous history' should have met because they both happened to be going for water at the same time. 'We must assume,' he says, 'that both were busy finding out what they could about each other's forces.'

But not all the Romans used espionage as cleverly as they might have done. Although Julius Caesar first introduced it into Britain when he invaded us in 55 BC, he refused to establish a secret service at home in Rome. If he had done so, perhaps Brutus might never have murdered him. There is a climate of opinion which has persisted right down to our own time, until we were rudely awakened from it, that espionage isn't 'quite nice', 'not really for gentlemen', and all that sort of thing. . . . 'Dash it, it's like opening another chap's letters!' as one former public-school boy British commander complained before the start of the Second World War. Of course it is. Perhaps if Julius Caesar had opened a few of the other chaps' letters in time he wouldn't have needed to beware the Ides of March.

Interestingly enough, though, in his time the Roman Empire was beginning to make use of more unorthodox methods of communication: Frontinus mentions pigeons as being in frequent use and so were trained swallows, a form of transport borrowed from ancient China.

Thus we can see that the ancient world had already planted the seeds of the tree that would spread its branches over our own time. All it needed was cultivation.

Opinions are divided as to whether King Alfred really did burn any cakes. He might well have done so: he had ample opportunities, particularly when he was in hiding. For he spent many years in hiding. He didn't waste those years in mourning over the past. He planned constructively for the future. And he did this by the judicious use of espionage!

He was the pioneer of the English secret service. And he played the minstrel to spy upon his enemies.

He first became king at the age of twenty-two. But he lost the throne to the invading Danes and then threw in his lot with a band of strolling players from whom he learnt a great many useful arts like playing the harp, acrobatics and juggling. Minstrels and harpers weren't fighting men, and they were allowed to enter armed camps unchallenged. At that time they were never questioned, nor did anyone ever raise the possibility that they could be spies.

It was when Alfred went into the camp of Guthrun the Dane that his undercover work produced results. It was his harp that opened the doors for him. While he played and was entertained with the other minstrels, Alfred kept his ears open and his mouth shut and made mental notes of the drunken boastings in the great hall and the idle gossip of the court. The upshot was that he returned to his retreat at Athelney with a plan for action.

On 11 May 878, he was ready. The Danes were unfit for sustained battle, as he had calculated that they would be, and with his loyal followers at his side it was only a matter of time before Guthrun surrendered.

King Alfred is the only ruler on record who is known to have tumbled and harped his way to victory.

It was the Mongols, under Genghis Khan, who first used mercenaries – soldiers who sold their services to the highest bidder – as spies. This resulted in a very efficient military secret service. The mercenary spies brought their own military knowledge with them. The Mongols also recruited local merchants from the countries through which they marched.

The great Khan, though, could be ruthless with enemy infiltrators. His code of Mongol laws, the Yassa, expressly stated, 'Spies, false witnesses, all men given to infamous vices, and black sorcerers, are condemned to death.' Thou shalt not suffer a witch to live, nor a spy it seems. This reminds us of the Russian SMERSH, meaning 'death to spies'.

The much-married Henry VIII allowed first Cardinal Wolsey and then Thomas Cromwell to run his secret service. Cromwell particularly had a 'police state' mentality and made many enemies.

Cromwell, like his descendant Oliver was to do later, covered England with spies and informers to such an extent that it was said that 'a scorpion lay beneath every stone'. There is a famous old saying, 'Which came first, the plotter or the spy?' When you have a lot of spies, you have a lot of people plotting against them, just as the reverse applies. The Tudors were masters at plotting, so the need for spies was great; and as more and more spies proliferated, so the need to plot against them grew. It was a vicious circle.

This was the climate into which Sir Francis Walsingham,

the first great architect of the British secret service, emerged. Born in 1530, the same year that Thomas Cromwell established his 'scorpion under every stone', his powers of organization, observation and analysis exactly fitted him for the role of spymaster. Walsingham was the true founder of the departments which were to evolve into MI5 and MI6 for intelligence and counter-intelligence.

There were enough plots against the life of Queen Elizabeth I to keep him more than occupied during his time of power. Philip of Spain, who was implicated in a great many of them, is said to have complained that his secret plans for conquering England were taken to Elizabeth by Walsingham's agents, read by her and then sent back to Spain where they were circulated as gossip in his own court before he had time to hand them officially to his ministers!

Not that Walsingham had much money to play around with. The meanness of Elizabeth is well documented and little enough was allocated on espionage. But money meant little to Walsingham and when he died it was in sickness and poverty, still owed money by the Crown.

Walsingham had inherited a rough-and-ready espionage system from his predecessor William Cecil, Lord Burghley, who had recommended to the queen Walsingham's appointment as principal secretary to the council. Burghley was Elizabeth's powerful lord treasurer, but he wasn't very interested in espionage. His system worked, up to a point, but Walsingham, faced with so many plots, refined and sharpened it – with Burghley's full approval.

The plots Walsingham had to contend with centred round Mary Stuart, Queen of Scots, who had been captured and imprisoned by Elizabeth. Mary was a Catholic, and the party of which she was the focal point wanted to see a

Catholic sovereign back on the throne of England. (Elizabeth's sister, also called Mary and her predecessor as queen of England, had been a staunch Catholic, and had married Philip of Spain.) Scarcely a month passed without some attempt to rescue her. In 1586 the famous Babington conspiracy took place. Anthony Babington, a 'young man of family and fortune', and a Jesuit priest named John Ballard were joined by several other conspirators, all sworn to shoot or stab Elizabeth when she was alone, or only in the company of her ladies-in-waiting.

Unfortunately for Queen Mary, Babington revealed the whole plot to her in a letter which, like all the rest, passed through Walsingham's hands. At the time Mary was kept a close prisoner at Chartley and she had evolved her own system of smuggling mail out of her quarters. Each week a brewer from Burton delivered a barrel of beer. He would then collect the empty barrel and the Queen's mail would be hidden in the empty barrels. What neither Mary nor her conspirators knew however was that the brewer was Walsingham's man; every letter was copied and read by the spymaster.

The promising young playwright Christopher Marlowe was also involved with Walsingham. He is considered by some critics as Shakespeare's greatest rival.

Oddly enough, Marlowe was recruited to act as a spy while still an undergraduate at Cambridge. (We'll see parallels to this when we come to look at the careers of the Foreign Office spies of our own time, Burgess, Maclean, Philby and Blunt.) The background to this centred round the Duke of Guise. As well as being the Scottish queen's uncle by marriage, he was leader of the orthodox Catholics in France and was continually devising ways of rescuing his niece and placing her on the English throne. With the object of recruiting Englishmen to help him, he used the Jesuit seminary at Rheims to offer extravagant hospitality to English students (a seminary is a college of religious instruction where men study to become Catholic priests). Marlowe had performed several small services for Walsingham and now he was asked by the spymaster to go to Rheims to find out what was going on.

There is no record that tells us whether or not Walsingham was happy with the information that the young man sent back. But at some point Marlowe changed his loyalties. Perhaps he began to study the Jesuit teachings. At any rate after a few more years he had become involved himself in a plot to depose Elizabeth and one of his fellow conspirators was the great Sir Walter Raleigh.

On the night of 30 May 1593 Marlowe received a summons telling him to go to the house of the Widow Bull on Deptford Strand, and when he got there he was shown into a room where three men were waiting. He must have known Mistress Bull quite well, because apparently he didn't question the message.

The three men were Robert Poley, Francis Sheers and Ingram Frazer. They were all Walsingham's agents. Poley and Frazer blocked the door when the young man tried to escape, and Frazer stabbed him in the eye with a poignard, a small dagger. The story then went round that Marlowe had been killed accidentally in a brawl over a woman in a Thamesside tavern, but rumours of mysterious and very different circumstances of Marlowe's death began a month later when Frazer was granted a free pardon for the murder and it was learned that Poley had been steward to Walsingham's daughter, Lady Sydney, the wife of the poet and courtier Sir Philip Sydney.

Of course to this day the mystery of Marlowe's death and what lay behind it remains. If Walsingham believed him to be implicated in a plot against Elizabeth, why wasn't he arrested in the normal way? Did he know too much about the spymaster's own methods? Certainly Walsingham was suspected of rigging evidence on a number of occasions, one of which was Mary's own trial, before she was finally executed in 1587. She herself accused him in court but his dramatic denial was flung out defiantly in front of everyone. 'God is my witness that as a private person I have done nothing unworthy of an honest man, and as a secretary of state, nothing unbefitted of my duty.' The question is exactly how much he considered to lie within the area of his duty.

Mary's death stirred Philip of Spain to action. Walsingham had known for some time that he had been building a vast fleet of ships in which to attack England, and many of Walsingham's spies had actually been working on the construction of those very ships, as carpenters, ropemakers and so on. It was these very same agents who helped to provide the advance information that enabled the British navy to defeat the Armada, as the Spanish fleet was called.

But the Tudor monarchs weren't known for their gratitude, and Elizabeth was no exception. Walsingham's day of usefulness was drawing to its close. The effect of his work, and perhaps more importantly, his ideas on the possibilities of espionage would be long-lasting and incalculable, but his health was bad and his days were numbered. At the time of his death the queen owed him well over £5000 for services rendered. He didn't care about money for himself, and the careful queen played upon that fact.

A seventeenth-century biographer said of him:

His head was so strong that he could look into the depths of men and business, and dive into the whirlpools of state. Dextrous he was in finding a secret; close in keeping it. His conversation was insinuation and reserved, he saw every man, and none saw him.

A relative of Lord Burghley and another member of the Cecil family, Robert, later the first Lord Salisbury, took over the secret service, but maintained it with none of the enthusiasm and energy of the great spymaster.

Christopher Marlowe was not the only literary man who dabbled in spying. In his time he had several talented rivals. His friend Matthew Roydon had mysterious truck with Elizabeth's successor to the throne, James I. Even Ben Jonson, author of the play *Bartholomew Fayre,* was a secret agent of the English Government, some biographers affirm. (When one is dealing with facts that are essentially secret it is not always possible to be absolutely certain and one must step warily, qualifying a great many statements.) The Scots poet William Fowler went to work for Walsingham in Scotland, while Anthony Monday, actor and playwright, went to Rome to spy upon the English seminary there, as his 'English Romayne Life' testifies. Later he toiled with a will in the public torture chamber! Elizabeth's personal physician, Dr Lopez, was believed to be a spy; some say he was the inspiration for Shylock in Shakespeare's *The Merchant of Venice.* Sadly there is no record that the Bard himself was ever caught up in spying, but so little is known about his life, particularly certain periods of it, that the question Was Shakespeare a Spy? could form the basis for some amusing research.

When we come to discuss present-day spies, we'll see that

in most cases celebrated spies are linked together in various ways. This was also true in earlier times. The figures who form the link between Sir Francis Walsingham and perhaps the most famous espionage story of all time, particularly amongst British children, were Robert Poley and Thomas Phelips. Phelips was Walsingham's chief decoder of intercepted letters, and the great man relied on his skill constantly.

It was his son, also called Thomas Phelips, one of England's first private detectives, who found out about the Gunpowder Plot. He had opened an agency for commercial espionage with that very same Robert Poley who had been implicated in the murder of Christopher Marlowe. It seems to have been purely by chance that he came to hear of a plot to kill King James. James himself, despite being the son of that Queen Mary who died for the Catholic faith, was himself staunchly Protestant. So when Elizabeth died childless and the House of Stuart succeeded the House of Tudor, the subversive plots instigated by the disappointed Catholics just went on.

Thomas Phelips Junior set about quietly making his own investigations and certain names were discovered. Robert Catesby, John and Christopher Wright, Thomas Percy, and one Guido – anglicized to Guy – Fawkes. So the great Gunpowder Plot of 1605 came to light (if you'll forgive the pun). The brother of Sir Thomas, Sir Edward Phelips, a noted lawyer, played a prominent part in the subsequent trial.

Robert Catesby, the instigator of the plot, was forced to bring in more conspirators from outside than he would have wished, because he ran short of money. One of those he approached for extra funds was Sir Francis Tresham,

noble of a prominent Catholic family. Catesby wasn't to
know that Tresham would have an attack of conscience and
warn his brother-in-law Lord Monteagle, who was due to
be present at the House of Lords when the gunpowder was
timed to explode, to stay away. Lord Monteagle himself
was thought to be a spy for the Crown, in the pay of Robert
Cecil, Walsingham's successor. He had originally been a
Catholic himself, but had turned his coat when James came
to the throne. Catesby believed he was still loyal to the old
cause, but paid dearly for his mistake when eventually
Monteagle revealed the whole plot.

Even if he hadn't have done so, Thomas Phelips had
come to his own conclusions. As everyone knows, the plot
was quite simply to blow up the Houses of Parliament and
everyone in it when the king would be speaking. To Guido
Fawkes was allocated the honour of lighting the fuse. But
armed men were waiting for him in the cellars. He was
seized, put to the rack and tortured, but refused to reveal
the names of his fellow conspirators until he learned that
they had given themselves away by staging an armed revolt.

It's a romantic tale, full of swashbuckling intrigue, that
perhaps, and perhaps not, has justified its continued cele-
bration every 5 November, the one historical date that
every child knows. Apart from bonfires and fireworks
throughout the land on that date, every day even now on
which Parliament assembles, a body of the Yeomen of the
Guard gathers in the House of Lords and then, lamps in
hand and halberds at the ready, searches the vaults and
cellars. So far they have always found everything in order,
so they return upstairs, make their reports and are
rewarded with a meal of bread, cheese and beer.

In 1704 Daniel Defoe, the great author of *Robinson Crusoe*, wrote a long paper which he called 'A Scheme for General Intelligence'. It was an instruction on how to seize power and establish a police state. 'Intelligence,' he wrote, 'is the soul of public business.' He summed up counter-intelligence equally concisely. 'For as intelligence is the most useful to us, so keeping our enemies from intelligence among us is as valuable a head.'

This was the scheme that Defoe put forward for the healthy maintainance of espionage. Each area in a country was to be allocated to a secret agent who was to send regular reports to his government on everything that happened in his area. Defoe also advised the keeping of dossiers on everyone of importance, so that potential troublemakers could be rounded up at the first sign of an emergency.

On the strength of this pamphlet Defoe became a paid government spy. Yet he never wrote about his real-life missions. Discretion triumphed, which is very frustrating for the rest of us. One reference is made to 'a special service in which I had run as much risk of my life as a grenadier upon a counterscarp'. This could have referred to a journey he made to Scotland in 1706, when he was sent to report on the feelings of the Scots on the controversial proposal to unite the English and Scottish parliaments. (He was ostensibly an author collecting material, rather than a spy.)

This thorny question has come up again during the present reign of Mrs Thatcher's government, you may recall. Who says that history does not repeat itself!

Queen Anne was on the throne during Defoe's career as a spy and she was very irritated by another political pamphlet he wrote called, 'The Shortest Way with Dissenters'. The shortest way with the writer, dissenter or not, was to fine him, put him in the pillory and then imprison him. Defoe complained constantly and bitterly about the meanness of his spymasters, who sent him on dangerous missions and then refused to pay him adequately for the risks he took.

Apart from a few fortunate exceptions, spies have always been badly paid and secret agents frequently die poor, disillusioned and disappointed. A spy may have chosen his profession because of the strength of his political beliefs or because he is being blackmailed for some past indiscretion; but normally he mustn't expect to make much money out of it. If he does so expect, he is speedily undeceived.

In the eighteenth century an efficient intelligence machine was finally accepted as an essential ingredient of home and foreign policy, fully as important as the army or the navy. The powerful Duke of Marlborough, ancestor of Winston Churchill, established the finest practical organization in Europe. From now on it could only grow larger.

In France, the Emperor Napoleon was the first to use what has now become a common ploy in espionage negotiations. What he did was to sign an order to intern British civilians, perfectly innocent of any war crimes, but whose one claim to suspicion was that they had been resident in France for some years at the time when France and England went to war. So all men between the ages of sixteen and eighty were rounded up and placed in detention; this made it possible to bargain for their release when England had some genuine prisoners-of-war – innocent tourists could be used as pawns in the war game. When we come to look at

Cold War spies, we'll see how the KGB adopted, and adapted, this procedure. . . .

Napoleon can be credited with three innovations that have contributed to modern warfare: internment of foreigners, the concentration camp and the system of one-way spy barter.

Espionage really needed a war on a global scale to prove how sophisticated its techniques had now become. And in 1914 it got one.

3
Spies in the First World War

Spies aren't normally executed in peacetime. But during a time of war, things are different. The penalty for espionage then is to face a firing squad . . . unless a spy is a civilian, in which case he or she may have to face the humiliation of the gallows. The Rosenbergs in America were put to death in the electric chair.

The first German spy caught at the beginning of the First World War was Karl Lody. Before he was shot by a platoon of the Grenadier Guards he was imprisoned in the Tower of London, mainly because the authorities were at a loss to know where else to put him. He was a German citizen, so had not betrayed his country. As such he was a hero rather than a criminal. Before facing the firing squad, the Provost Marshal invited him to his quarters and offered him a glass of wine, stretching out his hand and saying, 'I want to shake the hand of a brave man.'

This attitude towards spies and spying wore off, however, and later spies were treated with scant ceremony. Nowadays agents often defect to the countries to which they sold their secrets, or are exchanged for other spies. If they are subjects of the countries they have spied against, they can languish in prison for long periods if their sentences aren't reduced in the normal way. Unless capital punishment is reintroduced, this state of affairs can go on indefinitely.

In 1914 the British MI5 had been in existence for five years. Although its total stength was only four officers, three investigators and seven clerks, it had established close ties with Special Branch of Scotland Yard and could call upon all the uniformed police forces of Great Britain. The prejudice against espionage services as being 'ungentle-manly' meant that very little money was available; it wasn't the best attitude for maintaining efficiency, either.

A fortnight before war was declared, there were twenty-seven civilian spies in England for Germany and most of them had been living here for many years. Dr Karl Craves was already in prison, having been arrested in Glasgow in 1912 and tried and sentenced in Edinburgh. Gustav Stein-hauer, who wrote an autobiography with the duly modest title, *Steinhauer, the Kaiser's Master Spy* – his opinion, if nobody else's – travelled round England warning his fellow agents that war was coming. There was Kronauer in Walthamstow, Shaffmann in Exeter, Otto Weigels in Hull, Georg Kiener and various others. Steinhauer sent all of them a postcard on which was a coded warning. This was hardly the action of a master spy, as he claimed to be, particularly as he suspected that some of them were being watched, which indeed they were.

As a result of his tip-off, most of the agents got away safely to Germany, including Steinhauer himself. However some weren't so lucky, and a total of twenty-four spies were requested to accompany polite police officers in the early hours of 5 August. It is said that because of this round-up, no news whatever of Britain's mobilization reached Germany.

'Am I surrounded by dolts?' the Kaiser stormed. 'Why have I never been told that we have no spies in England?' This wasn't strictly true of course. It only seemed true.

Britain's trump card was naval intelligence, as befits an island people. This of course was before the days of aerial reconnaissance. Naval intelligence could be swift and deadly, though it was helped sometimes by luck. Here's an example.

A few hours after the declaration of war, the British cable ship *Telconia* put to sea for a destination just off the Dutch coast, found and winched up to the surface the submarine cable carrying German telegraph communications with the outside world, and cut it. Several hundred yards of cable were then reeled in and the cable cut again, making the damage irreparable. This forced Germany to use radio or send messages by enemy-controlled cable. So far so good, but for the exploit to be totally successful, it was necessary to learn how to read German signals.

This was where luck stepped in. On 26 August the German light cruiser *Magdeburg* ran aground in thick fog and was attacked by two Russian warships. Among the casualties picked up by the Russians was a German seaman clutching a heavy book. The man was obviously dying and one of his last thoughts had been to save the book. His rescuers discovered that it contained the German naval code which the Russian High Command very kindly offered to the Admiralty. A destroyer was especially sent by Winston Churchill, then First Sea Lord, to fetch it from Murmansk. (The Russians were a little more cooperative then than they are now.)

This code provided the key that naval intelligence needed to read German messages sent by cable. Luck stepped in a second time to provide the key to another code. A young German consul named Wilhelm Wassmuss, stationed in Persia, decided instead of returning to Berlin on the outbreak of war to ride off into the hills with the object of organizing local tribesmen and fighting a guerilla war to sabotage British oil interests in the Persian Gulf. He was the German equivalent of Lawrence of Arabia, who tried to make trouble for the Turks.

The British put a huge price on the head of Wassmuss. Accounts vary on the exact amount. Some say it started at £3000 and went up to £25,000. Others that it reached a ceiling of £50,000. But whatever the truth, the fact remains that he was considered an extremely valuable catch and, equally, that he was never betrayed by any of his associates - peasants or tribesmen. It was said that no one believed anyone was worth that much!

Pursued relentlessly by British patrols, he once had to abandon his baggage when he was caught by surprise and forced to run. Then it was learned that he was offering a considerable sum for the return of a trunk that he believed had been taken by local inhabitants. But the British had found it and when they opened it they were amazed to find that it contained a copy of the top-secret German diplomatic code.

Germany supplied Wassmuss with enough gold and ammunition to let him continue with his sabotage activities until she began to lose the war. Then when he could no longer pay his Persian agents and saboteurs, he was assigned a monthly salary of 300 rupees. After the collapse of Germany's military activities in the Orient, Wassmuss disappeared from the scene. He was never captured by the British and he never again emerged into prominence. Strictly speaking he wasn't a spy at all. His main interest was in sabotage, but this lone romantic figure didn't stop at espionage and he certainly employed spies.

One of the main problems for England was how to get agents into Europe. Aircraft flew over at night, dropping some in and picking up others, but taking off in moonlit fields was dangerous and many men and machines were lost. Agents began to use parachutes, but the Germans were suspicious of planes droning about behind their lines at night without dropping bombs, so reception committees were arranged. Then free balloons were tried. Agents carrying wireless sets drifted silently across enemy lines when the wind was favourable; surprisingly enough, many of them landed more or less where they were supposed to.

The wireless sets that were taken in were primitive and not particularly efficient. It was still early days for radio. To send messages pigeons were still used, as they had been all those centuries ago by the Romans. The birds got to where they were going all right, but were limited in how much they could carry. And the Germans were liable to shoot, without asking too many questions, anyone who had a pigeon in a basket or a cage.

More and more unlikely methods were used for getting information from one point to another. For example the border between Holland and Belgium had been sealed off, so somebody had the bright idea of knotting messages inside rubber contraceptives, tucking them into sliced-open potatoes or other roots and tossing them to agents on the other side of the barrier!

The twin problems of decoding signals and methods of communication occupied British intelligence to a very large extent during the First World War. Because espionage and counter-espionage had grown so fast in the exceptional circumstances of a world war, ruthlessness gave rise to many 'dirty tricks'. Perhaps the prize for the most ingenious and merciless disposal of an enemy should go to Richard Meinertzhagen, a British intelligence officer stationed on the coast of German East Africa, who discovered that an Arab living on the shore of Lake Tanganyika was an enemy spy.

Meinertzhagen wrote a brief letter to him and, thanking him for services rendered, enclosed a sum of money. He sent the letter through a courier that he suspected of being a double agent. As he had guessed he would, the courier took it straight to the German commander. Since nobody really trusts a spy, as Napoleon pointed out, the unfortunate Arab was taken out of his hut and shot without being asked for an explanation. The trick was repeated during the Palestine campaign in 1917, when Meinertzhagen wished to get rid of a Turkish spymaster whose operations had been too successful. A similar letter and sum of money was sent, the enemy spy was eliminated, and the Turks and Germans thereby destroyed their own source of intelligence.

Most people have heard the name of Mata Hari and to many she symbolizes the beautiful spy, sinuous and tempting. Perhaps they've seen the famous film starring Greta Garbo, who played her very much according to the popular image. But who was she really? And was she as beautiful as she is made out to be?

One book I came across really wasn't sure. 'She wasn't beautiful,' we find stated baldly. Yet, a little further on, 'For her beauty alone she was unforgettable, as many have testified.' Admittedly these words were written by two different writers, but – you pays your money . . . Certainly contemporary photographs don't flatter her.

Let's get rid of the legend first, the legend that is almost totally untrue. She brought about no bloody defeats, no glorious victories to great armies. She trifled with the destinies of no great nations, outwitted no presidents or prime ministers, duped no monarchs or nobility of Europe, nor did she face death particularly courageously when she was unmasked.

These stories were allegedly created by the French military high command, nourished by officially leaked but invented secrets, and blown up to mythic proportions by sensation-writers (any genuine woman spy is now automatically 'a second Mata Hari'). At that time the French authorities were anxious to find a scapegoat for the inept behaviour of their own top officers.

Mata Hari's real name was Margaretha Gertruda Zelle, and she was born in Leewwarden, Holland, on 7 August 1876. She married a young Dutch officer named MacLeod, home on leave from the East Indies, and she returned with him when his leave was over. Her child was born there.

But she had no feeling for domesticity and the marriage ended in divorce. She returned alone to Europe and decided to try her hand as a dancer. While living in Indonesia she had become fascinated with the erotic temple dances, and now determined to put that interest to good use. Rechristening herself Mata Hari (Eye of the Morning), her dancing exhibition was an instant success, enhanced probably by the fact that she was almost nude. Her audiences were exclusively men and she often gave private performances, as well as more substantial favours, to her enthusiastic audiences.

People disagree as to whether she was really a spy at all. If she was, she seems to have been loyal only to herself. She lived a flamboyant life as a dancer and had many influential lovers; it is more than likely that some at least were indiscreet enough to discuss confidential topics with her.

She was believed to have attended espionage school for a term in 1910, but her notoriety began – and ended – in one year, 1917, when she was taken off a boat bound from Spain to Holland and transported to France on a trumped-up charge. She was accused of smuggling news to the Germans about the mutinies in the French army, the anger and resentment of the French troops against their leaders being an inconvenient thorn in the side of the generals. Poor Mata Hari happened to be in the wrong place at the right time, and as a matter of expediency was sentenced to be shot.

During her trial the prosecution alleged that she had become a German spy before the war, with the code number, H21. The French had intercepted telegrams from a German masterspy, Wilhelm Canaris, in which she was referred to as H21. And it was discovered that orders were given for payments to be made to her as H21.

She admitted that she was indeed H21 and that she did receive payments through Canaris. But she asserted that the payments were for her services as his mistress. It sounds plausible. Canaris couldn't afford to pay her from his income, so he placed her on his payroll. Today businessmen do that all the time.

This story was laughed out of court as 'fantastic' by the prosecution. Nevertheless while Mata Hari was on trial, the French intelligence service was using a woman spy who was securing payment from the Germans under exactly similar circumstances.

She is more interesting for our purposes than Mata Hari, because it was established beyond doubt that she was a genuine spy. Her name was Marthe Richer, and she was one of the first woman aviators. After the death of her husband, a French officer killed in action early in 1916, she was recruited as a spy by one of his friends. This was a Captain Ledoux and he sent her to Madrid with orders that she become the mistress of a German naval attaché stationed there. During her stay there she met Mata Hari, who at that time was living with von Kalle, the German military attaché. Marthe Richer later stated that she had no suspicion that Mata Hari, or Lady MacLeod as she called herself, was supposed to be a spy.

Marthe Richer sent Ledoux valuable information on German submarine refuelling points on the Spanish coast and also details of the secret routes used by German agents through the Pyrenees into France. In 1933 she was rewarded with the Legion of Honour.

Getting back to poor Mata Hari and her trial, it is pretty well accepted now that it was a travesty of justice. Here is an example of the false evidence that was used.

This time she was supposed to be spying for the French. Her loyalties changed with the wind (this latter part is probably true; they depended on who her lover was at the time!). She was supposed to have said that two German U-boats planned to land arms at the Moroccan port of Mehadiya so that Moroccan rebels would be able to harass

French forces. She had passed this information, it was alleged, to divert suspicion from her anti-French activities, when she realized she was being watched. It wasn't until years later that law students going through the trial records discovered that there was no Moroccan port of Mehadiya and that neither French nor German U-boats were ever seen off the Moroccan coast!

Mata Hari's end was futile, whether she had ever been a spy or not. She was shot by a firing squad on 17 October 1917. But her legend persists.

There weren't many successful German spies operating in England during the First World War, but a brilliant exception was Jules Silber.

It was Silber alone who never put a foot wrong. Other agents made quick trips to Britain and managed to return with scraps of information, but it was Silber who lived and worked in enemy territory for years, sending a constant flow of invaluable information to Germany. He has been called one of the most consistently effective spies of all time.

He worked in one of the major branches of counter-espionage, like Kim Philby in the Second World War. Before coming to England he had travelled all over the world, and had lived in South Africa where he had fought for the British in the Boer War.

You didn't need a passport to travel before 1914, but documents proving his services to Britain, and a number of influential contacts, got him a job in postal censorship. The fact that he was a German hadn't meant a great deal to him before the war, but now his patriotism was aroused. He was very much a freelance and a lone wolf, and was answerable to no one but himself and Germany. He said later:

The catastrophe which had befallen Germany had aroused me from the indifference with which I had regarded its political affairs and fortunes. I felt myself suddenly bound to the country, which though I scarcely knew it, was my native land, and I was carried away by a passionate, irresistible urge to serve it now that it was in need.

He couldn't have chosen better than the postal censorship department, crucial as it was to Germany. Every day he read a mass of letters and every day he pieced together all sorts of information which he sent out from a room he had hired on the other side of London. Here he photographed material, wrote his reports and sent out envelopes marked 'passed by the censor'. He left stubs of concert and theatre tickets around to explain his absences to his landlady.

As well as passing information, Silber performed small but useful acts of sabotage. Blueprints for new ordinance (guns) passed through his hands. Burning ash from his pipe here, an ink blot there, and the drawings were useless! At times he even managed to lose them altogether.

Another way in which he threw spanners into the works was through overzealousness, devotion to red tape above and beyond the call of duty. Ships arriving had to have all their papers cleared by the censor before unloading could begin. Silber saw to it that as many people as possible had to examine every document; the delays he caused sometimes amounted to days. This affected the flow of supplies quite considerably. He later estimated that he had caused holdups equal to 400,000 tons of freight space in a year.

But these were only small and petty actions. He was involved in larger schemes as well. His greatest discovery was the British plan for Q-ships, the carefully disguised armed merchantmen which were to blow so many German submarine raiders out of the water. A young girl wrote to her sister in Canada saying that their brother had been decorated for gallantry in action while serving in a new type of ship that would 'soon end the U-boat campaign'. She even gave the name of the port where the ship was lying.

In his capacity as official government censor, Silber called on the girl personally to reproach her for her indiscretion. While he talked to her like a father and she promised that it would never happen again, he was able to collect all the information he wanted!

When the war ended, and the department was disbanded, Silber was congratulated personally by the Director of Military Intelligence for his sterling work in the department. In a letter he wrote:

I wish to thank you for the work you have done in my directorate. The Censorship has inevitably worked to a large extent in the dark, and the public has even now little appreciation of the pressure which this weapon has enabled us to exert on the enemy, or on the part it played in winning the war. You may however be sure that in the General Staff there is no lack of appreciation of the importance of the work to which you have given your services.

There is no record that the writer of this rather turgid letter ever found out the truth!

Silber needed to stay at his post, so he continually refused promotion, giving the excuse that his health would not allow him greater responsibility. Of course there was nothing wrong with his health at all, and to back up his excuse he had to take drugs. They were effective, but too much so, and he had a complete breakdown after the strain under which he had been living was finally removed. (This is an occupational hazard for all those engaged in espionage.)

He went on living in England till 1925, waiting for the time when he could return to Germany. He picked up occasional work as a researcher for film companies, but it must have been a bitter pill to swallow that the victory for which he had worked so hard didn't come after all. When he did get home at last, he wrote a book on his experiences as a German spy. The book must have proved a nasty shock to a great many people. He was a volunteer, succeeding where so many agents carefully chosen by the Fatherland had failed.

We'll end this brief look at the First World War with an eyewitness account of how a spy was caught and a possible assassination attempt on King George V foiled. The story-teller is Edwin T. Woodhall of the American secret service.

During the war King George V made several trips to France to visit HQ, hospitals and the battlefields.

Needless to say these journeys were a source of very great anxiety to the General Staff and all concerned with the King's safety. Every precaution was taken to guard His Majesty. A selecte *he* ctive, generally from the ranks of the Intelligence police, was always attached to him as a personal guard. As bad luck would have it, during these visits there was nearly always some unpleasant incident, and I remember one occasion when a plot to assassinate His Majesty was defeated in the nick of time by the sagacity and intelligence displayed by a private in a Scottish regiment.

On that occasion the King was staying at a château which was used sometimes as a temporary HQ by Sir Douglas Haig. At the time of the King's visit the British Commander-in-Chief was established on his famous train in a siding only a short distance from the château, and here His Majesty dined and lunched frequently.

It was arranged for the King to visit certain hospitals and to review certain divisions of troops newly-arrived in France. On the day before the big review, word came to the Inter-Allied Secret Service that there was obviously a serious leakage of information. The enemy were getting most accurate intelligence as to the movements of troops in the vicinity of the place where the King intended to hold his review.

Special efforts were made to trace the leakage, and at the request of my Chief of Intelligence, I went down to the suspected district and made a few independent enquiries. After careful work I learned of an old Flemish woman who seemed to be living far more comfortably than the present hard circumstances warranted to one in the war zones. I detailed one of my best men to watch her. After nightfall he saw her leave her cottage and make her away along a shell-torn path to a ruined château.

She entered and he followed. He had two assistants at hand, and as soon as the old woman came out of the building, he made his way up the stairs leading to a shell-broken turret.

Partly demolished by long-range gunfire, the steps were unsafe, and great care had to be exercised lest he fall through a hole in the side. He neared the top. Twice he heard the hoot of an owl, but paid no attention. He could see the stairs above him. He was perhaps seven feet from the top, when a vicious crack, a flash and the heat of flame instinctively made him duck. He saw a pair of legs and grabbed at them. Crash! His assailant fell down the stairs. A groan. My man struck a match. He saw lying beneath him a young, thick-set man, unconscious and bleeding freely from a wound on the side of the head. Calling his comrade by name several times, he received no answer.

Striking another match, he saw by the light another body – it was his comrade. He was dead. Shot through the heart.

The unconscious man was searched and an identity disc of a

German infantry regiment round his neck revealed him as a spy in disguise. A search of the top tower soon revealed the presence of a wireless signalling apparatus, and on his person were found details of the King's movements for the next three days.

Details of the King's tour were changed without notice, and the spy was shot following a court-martial.

This story really has everything.

4

Spies in the Second World War

Having won the 'war to end wars', the British, French and Americans demobilized their forces, reduced their intelligence services to a minimum and, by keeping that minimum on an extremely tight budget, left the field wide open for the Germans, the Japanese and the Russians. Germany in particular smarted under her defeat and lived for the moment when the army of the Fatherland could reap its vengeance. It needed an Adolf Hitler, and it got one.

One of the founder-members of the fast-rising Nazi Party was Hermann Lang. He went to America in the early thirties and got a job at the Norden engineering works on Long Island, from where he sent information back to Germany.

Soon after Hitler came to power in 1933 his spies and agents began operating busily. They belonged to the Abwehr, the German intelligence department specializing in overseas operations. One agent, whose cover name was Doctor Ranken, got in touch with Lang who was working on the new and very secret development of a bombsighting device for the US Air Force. When they met Lang handed over copies of all the blueprints. Later he went back to

Germany to see that they'd got it right when they started their own construction. Like Jules Silber, Lang was a free-lance who wanted no persuasion and not much payment. He did it for the glory of the Fatherland, although a 'present' was slipped into his hand by Marshal Hermann Goering, head of the Luftwaffe (the German air force.)

Lang returned to America and in due course Britain was bombed with the aid of the Norden bombsight. Admiral Wilhelm Canaris (he who had been involved with Mata Hari!) was now in charge of the Abwehr; he realized that as soon as a German plane was shot down and the Allies discovered that the Germans had the bombsight, Lang would be compromised, and his usefulness over. He tried to get him back to Germany, but was foiled by an FBI agent who had infiltrated the Abwehr. Lang was arrested in 1941, sentenced to ten years' imprisonment and released in 1950; he returned to Germany and got a job in a Bavarian factory.

The first large Soviet spy ring active in Europe was known as the Red Orchestra by German intelligence. Agents sent in floods of information from Vienna, Brussels, Berlin, Oslo, Madrid and Switzerland. The most prominent among them was Rudolph Roessler, who lived in Lucerne and had the codename Lucy. He was in close contact with a key member of Hitler's staff, who passed him details of practically every undertaking planned by the German high command, including the date, time, place and strength of the German invasion of Russia that would take place in 1941. Stalin had several confirmations of this information from various underground sources, but chose to ignore every one. As someone said during a BBC programme about the history of intelligence, Stalin was a typical paranoiac . . . he acted instantly to imagined dangers, but often ignored real ones.

It's amazing, and rather frightening, how often information sent by spies isn't believed until it's too late. Admittedly it has been known for inept agents to falsify material deliberately, just to show their spymasters and department heads that their continued presence is justified and that they are doing their job; but any information, however unlikely it may appear, is ignored at considerable danger. There are many cases where the course of history could have been changed if only notice had been taken in time.

The Yugoslav agent Dusko Popov, in his book *Spy, Counterspy,* claims that he gave details of the proposed Japanese attack on Pearl Harbor to J. Edgar Hoover, head of the FBI, well in advance, but that nothing was done. Hoover was a difficult and notorious man, whose years in authority had made him intolerant and may have led him to believe that he was infallible. Because he disliked Popov personally, and disapproved of the rather riotous life style favoured by the Yugoslav, he chose not to believe him.

Another spy who ferreted out advance German plans for a Russian invasion – surely one of the worst-kept secrets of the war – was Richard Sorge, a brilliant journalist who was able to wander in and out of the German Embassy in Japan, being what is called *persona grata* (acceptable personnel), and who ran a spy ring which penetrated the Japanese war cabinet. Sorge was able to send information to the Allies about Japan's own role in future hostilities, particularly concerning whether she would launch an offensive against eastern Russia or concentrate her efforts on the Pacific, which is what she eventually did.

Sorge was caught by the Japanese in 1944 and hanged,

believing right to the end that Stalin, for whom he worked, would save him. But Stalin lost interest when Sorge's usefulness was at an end. His faithful Japanese mistress took the gold fillings from his teeth after he was dead and had them made into a ring which she wore in his memory.

War always stimulates new technology and highly sophisticated methods of communication had been evolved since this had proved such a big problem in the First World War. Miniature photographic equipment made it possible to reduce a foolscap page of information to the size of a small punctuation mark, the microdot, and consequently ever more ingenious hiding places could be used.

A very important development indeed, the secrets of which were acquired by the British early on in the war, was the German Enigma machine. This turned a message into an unintelligible scramble before transmitting it in Morse.

The British knew about this wonder from an anti-German Pole who worked on the construction of the machine before the war. So a number of wireless operators, code-decipherers and intelligence officers formed a special highly trained team at what was called Station X based at Bletchley Park, a Victorian mansion in Buckinghamshire. Station X brought off a large number of outstanding and invaluable intelligence coups.

In order to break the Enigma code, a decoder had to be developed and this was called Ultra. Regarded as the most valuable source of information of the whole war, Ultra was jealously guarded. It decoded the top-secret signals sent by the German high command, including plans for the 1941 Russian invasion, now called Operation Barbarossa.

Ultra led to the breaking of many German codes at

Bletchley Park. One coup that the Station X team brought off was the breaking of a German U-Boat code, which enabled the Royal Navy to hunt, find and sink German submarines faster than they could be replaced. Another was the reading of a message from Field Marshal Rommel to Field Marshal Kesselring, describing a trap laid for the victorious Eighth Army while they were being chased in the North African desert after the battle of El Alamein. Their supplies were to be cut off, thus paving the way for Rommel's own advance into Cairo.

Recruiting of the staff at Bletchley Park was based very firmly on academic achievements. The universities, particularly Oxford and Cambridge, were combed for promising graduates and undergraduates. Two categories whom they wanted particularly were those of good ability in foreign languages, and those studying Egyptology who had an interest and an ability for deciphering ancient hieroglyphics. It wasn't unknown, either, for schoolboys who had won classical scholarships and were waiting to go up to university, to find themselves under consideration for jobs in the cipher department.

Amongst those who joined the staff was a certain Anthony Blunt, whom we will meet again later. There was also Malcolm Muggeridge, who has some amusing tales to tell both about his time at Bletchley Park, and his career in intelligence generally.

A young naval officer was sacked, he tells us, because in an information report he had dared to criticize Admiral Doenitz, head of the German navy, as being 'very silly'. He was firmly reprimanded. It was not, he was told, for a mere lieutenant to criticize an admiral 'in any navy whatsoever' . . .

Mr Muggeridge has also mentioned the continuous search that went on for ingredients from which could be made the precious material called secret ink. This was what it sounds like: ink or its equivalent that could be faded out to invisibility and made to reappear again under the correct circumstances. Something, apparently, that was tried out and found to be effective was what Mr Muggeridge refers to as 'bird-shit'! This substance worked, and Mr Muggeridge relates the saga of one of his colleagues trying to attract birds to his balcony, and of early-morning forages into Hyde Park with a handkerchief at the ready to collect piles of pigeon droppings!

Faced with the attitude that could fire a lieutenant for daring to criticize an admiral, notwithstanding the fact that he was an enemy, the Bletchley Park team found themselves resented as a bunch of undergraduates and civilian amateurs by the more orthodox secret service chiefs. Even Winston Churchill, on one of his visits to Bletchley, is reported to have said; 'I told you to leave no stone unturned in your recruiting. I did not expect you to take me so literally.'

But despite what looks suspiciously like ingratitude, the Bletchley team got results. Discipline among the academics might have been informal, but the fact remains that the German services' Enigma code was broken continually from 1940 to 1945 and the contribution of Station X to the Allied victory was incalculable.

We've said elsewhere that Britain and America were careful about what secrets they shared with Russia, even during the wars against Germany. The secrets of codebreaker Ultra were shared with all the Allies except the Soviets.

Air photography was now widely used in espionage. One of the pioneers was Group Captain Winterbottom, who gives some amusing accounts of early problems. 'The original idea of doing something new in aerial photography originated from pioneers hanging wooden cameras out of cockpits going up and down the Rhine,' he says.

When they started, the photographers couldn't take photos above 8000 feet because of condensation on the camera lens. They just had to take three Leica cameras up the German coast and do the best they could. It was the Lockheed 14, with its heated cabin, that got rid of the condensation problem and made high-altitude aerial reconnaissance a practical proposition. Winterbottom and another pilot named Sydney Cotton went on reconnaissance missions over German and Italian targets before the official outbreak of war. When it came, this branch of espionage, under the Air Ministry, was based at Heston, with Sydney Cotton in charge. They used modified Spitfires, painted eggshell blue to blend in with the sky, and flew at 30,000 feet. It seems a far cry from today's spy satellites.

The decoder Ultra had a job to do on the home front as well as overseas. It helped MI5 track down German spies in Britain. In time-honoured tradition, some of them were then turned into double agents who fed back false information to Germany. British intelligence ran a highly complex system of double-cross, whose sole purpose was to confuse the German high command. In many cases so-called spies were really innocent dupes. The invincible Third Reich, the empire that Hitler told us would last a thousand years, to the end maintained its faith in its false agents, and even in its death throes requested them, pathetically, to keep in touch. . . . It never recognized its own betrayers.

The most spectacular result of this British James Bond operation was that it made possible what was called Operation Overlord – the D-Day Normandy landings which depended on complete control of sea and air and the deception of German high command, who were expecting it in the wrong place! They believed that the Allies would land further east, in the Pas de Calais.

One of the most celebrated ruses employed by MI5 to convince Germany that the landings would take place in the Pas de Calais rather than in Normandy gives a very good indication of its tactics. It was the case of 'Monty's Double'.

General Montgomery was known to be one of the principal commanders of the invasion forces and now the Germans began to notice that he was making more and more appearances around Gibraltar and South Africa, visiting British troops accompanied by the usual retinue of war correspondents and press photographers. The visits were leisurely and routine and could only mean to the gullible high command that no immediate invasion was planned.

In fact the visitor wasn't Monty at all, but an actor named M. E. Clifton-James, who looked so like him that he could have been his twin. Mr Clifton-James, commissioned into the Royal Army Pay Corps, later wrote a book on the deception, which was subsequently filmed. The title of book and film was *I Was Monty's Double*.

Another spectacular example of deception, also designed to confuse the Germans over the exact location of an Allied landing, this time involved southern Europe. The landing was to be made in Sicily but the Germans had to be made to believe that it would happen in Sardinia, with diversionary attacks in Greece. The incident became known as the case of the spy who never was, and this too became the subject of a feature film.

What happened was this. At the end of April 1943 the drowned body of Major William Martin, Royal Marines, was washed ashore in the Gulf of Cadiz. Chained to his wrist was a briefcase containing sealed envelopes and not far away floated a rubber dinghy, obviously from a ditched aircraft. The pockets of his uniform contained details of a sad little story.

There was an identity card, the kind of thing everyone had to carry during the war. There was a worn photograph of a girl and letters signed Pam, a jeweller's receipt for an engagement ring, ticket stubs from a London theatre, bus tickets, keys and a gentle letter from a bank manager about a slight overdraft. The Spanish authorities carried out a post mortem, and death by drowning was confirmed by the presence of water in the lungs of the dead man. It was known that the sympathies of the chief of the Spanish naval staff lay with Hitler, so consequently there was a delay of two weeks before the briefcase was handed over to the British ambassador.

In that time the contents had been copied and the envelopes carefully resealed by a German agent. But the British had painstakingly ensured that those contents were false information that the Allied invasion would take place in Sardinia.

The charade was played out. During the delay while the briefcase and its contents were being scrutinized, an urgent exchange of signals between British heads of departments was picked up. The exchanges took the form of agonized questions on what had happened to papers of great importance that had been in the possession of a courier named Major Martin.

The corpse was actually that of an unmarried civilian who had died in London of pneumonia – hence the water in the lungs – and it had been taken to the Spanish coast by submarine. The play-acting worked. The Germans regarded the finding of Major Martin as an incredible piece of luck. They redistributed their forces accordingly, but on 10 July the Allies landed in Sicily.

This elaborate hoax was engineered, as were so many others, by MI5. Naturally it was imperative that its home base remain a secret and for a time it occupied the buildings of Wormwood Scrubs, a prison in London. The prisoners were moved out.

It was rumoured that an old prison chaplain accustomed to preaching his regular Sunday sermons to the prisoners, a captive audience in every sense, went on under the new regime, conscientiously reminding his congregation, as was his custom, that they must go straight as soon as they had paid their debts to society and were released, and that they must try not to get into any more trouble. Perhaps in view of some of the less scrupulous activities of MI5, he was justified.

What spies have to tell us isn't always taken seriously, as we saw with Stalin and Operation Barbarossa, and Hoover and Pearl Harbor. This applies all the more when information is received anonymously.

This was exactly what happened in November 1940 when a document that became known as the Oslo Report was sent to the British naval attaché in the Norwegian capital. It was signed, 'A German scientist who wishes you well'; to this day nobody has discovered who he was.

The Oslo Report contained enough technical information about Germany's secrets to amaze even the most sceptical. New radar devices, gliders that flew themselves without the need for pilots, remote-controlled shells, new types of fuses and new designs for torpedoes – no one believed the document wasn't a plant. It seemed like the wildest fantasy but the scoffers were wrong. The Oslo Report was correct in every detail.

So was a warning sent to British intelligence officers by none other than Laurenti Beria himself, one of the most ruthless officers of the Russian KGB and soon to become its head. The information he sent seemed too far-fetched to be possible, yet this is just when intelligence should be at its most cautious. What he had to say was later confirmed by British aerial photographs taken in France. Beria informed Britain that Germany was building robot flying bombs for use against us. It wasn't till the first V-1s flew over London that his report was accepted as true, and by that time it was too late to do much about it.

Another spy who reported on the location of the V-1 factories was a colourful character named Eddie Chapman. Codenamed Zigzag, he began his career by deserting from the Coldstream Guards and taking up professional safe-breaking. He pioneered the use of gelignite. When it seemed that the police were about to catch up with him, he and his associates decided to hide out in Monte Carlo, making the journey via Jersey in the Channel Islands.

He was arrested by the Jersey police for practising his old profession and while he was serving a three-year prison sentence the Germans arrived to occupy the Channel Islands. (These islands were the only British territory that the Germans did occupy.)

When he was set free, Eddie Chapman made his way to the German secret service and offered them his services. He had by that time accumulated a healthy dossier of press cuttings which described his activities as a burglar in some detail, and the Germans were impressed. Unfortunately, while they were finally deciding whether or not to recruit this explosives expert, Chapman was arrested again, this time for black-market activities in Jersey's capital, St Helier. The illegal buying and selling of goods normally rationed, scarce, or unobtainable was known as the black market; most people supplemented their rations in some way by using its facilities. (Kids, ask your parents!)

German intelligence finally accepted Eddie Chapman and he was taken to France for training. His initiation began in a château near the River Loire. An instructor named Maurice Schmidt taught him how to operate a radio set and use Morse and other codes; a demolitions expert named Herbert Vosch enlarged on his knowledge of explosives – which didn't need much enlarging. Vosch boasted that he had assisted the IRA in an attempt to blow up Hammersmith Bridge before the war.

Eddie was now known as Fritz, an industrious pupil. He would be a saboteur as well as a spy and his target was the De Havilland aircraft factory at Hatfield, a few miles from London. In 1942 the plant was manufacturing a very effective little bomber named the Mosquito.

For the sum of £10,000 and £45 a month, Chapman agreed not only to blow up the factory but also to report back on troop movements, ranks and numbers of United States troops in Britain, and the location of anti-aircraft batteries.

Armed with a supply of detonators and a radio set, and

carrying all the right identification cards and currency, Eddie Chapman baled out over the Fen district. But MI5 were waiting for him. Ultra had done its usual stuff and radio messages announcing his arrival had been intercepted and deciphered. He would, they thought, serve excellently as a double agent and of course Chapman agreed. 'After all,' he said, 'I *am* on your side.'

The mock explosion at De Havilland's was one of the masterpieces of the war. Obviously it was necessary to fool German reconnaissance aircraft, so to create the necessary effect a team of stage designers from the Old Vic theatre at Waterloo was called in.

The results were masterly. Seen from the air, great cracks and holes in the walls had appeared, with rubble and broken girders all round. Newspapers even published mock reports and their editors were encouraged to criticize the inadequate security precautions that let these awful disasters happen.

The ace saboteur Fritz Graumann was awarded the Iron Cross for his exploits, the only Englishman to be singled out for such distinction in the Second World War. He was also paid in full by his German employer.

German intelligence next asked Chapman to report back on the V-1s; since the bombs flew without pilots, they wanted to know how accurate they were when they landed, how close to their targets they got. For this he was to be paid £100,000. But MI5 got to him first and Chapman diligently radioed back to Germany as much false information as he could on the positions of the bomb bursts. On every occasion the truth was doctored just sufficiently to ensure that the V-1 launchers made inaccurate corrections to the trajectory, sending the flying bombs to the less heavily populated areas of London. People still got killed, of course, but without Eddie Chapman's wool-pulling over the German eyes, the casualty rate would have been many times greater.

He survived the war and prospered, receiving a full pardon for any outstanding offences connected with his previous profession. He bought himself a Rolls Royce, and a health farm.

Simeon Rostovsky, a Russian journalist in Britain who broadcast regularly from the BBC in London and who was later revealed to be a Soviet spymaster, made this comment about the efficiency of Soviet espionage in Germany in 1941:

The Nazis can't cut down every tree in the Russian forest. Hundreds of them [Nazis, not trees] are killed every week behind their own lines. Guerrillas appear as if from nowhere, fulfil their assignments and vanish again. They know all about the Germans, their stations [HQs], their numbers and their officers. They have an intelligence service which is among the best in the world –

This is very true, as Britain and America have found to their costs. The infiltration abilities of the KGB are second to none.

But before we get on to the stern realities of the Cold War in our modern world, let's look, if only briefly, at another expert infiltrator, Mr Elias Bazna.

Like so many spies, Mr Bazna worked for money rather than for patriotism. Like Eddie Chapman he was daring and colourful, and like Eddie he escaped with his life at the end of the war.

His cover was blown by a member of the German

Foreign Office who appeared in Switzerland in August 1943 and handed over to American intelligence a mass of information, more than 2700 documents. This man's codename was George Wood and on Mr Wood's list of spies the name of Elias Bazna was writ large.

Bazna was valet to the British ambassador in Turkey, Sir Hughe Knatchbull-Hugessen, and his information was so revealing and valuable that at first it was thought to be a trap. The consensus of German opinion was that it couldn't possibly be genuine!

What he did was simplicity itself, because he was in the right place at the right time. And, after all, who bothers to take much notice of a valet?

But this valet was different, and had some very particular extra-curricular duties. He had impressions of all Sir Hughe's keys and at every convenient moment photographed the documents which his master was careless enough to bring up from his office and leave in his bedroom for leisurely examination.

Bazna soon convinced a contact in the German embassy named Moyzisch to pass his photographs on to the German foreign minister himself, von Ribbentrop. Von Ribbentrop's reaction was perhaps natural. He refused to believe that a mere servant could have access to such classified material as the list of British agents in Turkey, full details of plans discussed at Allied conferences, plans for the invasion of Europe and the key to the Allied diplomatic code. He told the German ambassador, Franz von Papen, that it was obviously a hoax, much too good to be true.

But von Papen wasn't so sure. The circumstances in which Cicero, as Bazna was codenamed, had acquired the information seemed plausible. So he sent Moyzisch to try to convince the head of the embassy security office, von Kaltenbrunner; he too was doubtful, but he agreed to play along and allocated to von Papen the sum of £200,000 in English notes to exploit Cicero. They couldn't convince von Ribbentrop, who resolutely refused to act on any information from that source.

In Switzerland the American who had been primed by the defector George Wood began to investigate Cicero; Bazna's contact, Moyzisch, got wind of the inquiries and warned him. His reaction was to gather up the banknotes which he kept under the carpet in his room – the payment he received for information had now grown to about £300,000 – and disappear.

Later he discovered that every note of money that he had been paid by the Germans was counterfeit! (Its source was a printing plant in Berlin; the fake money was to be used in the event of a German victory to debase British currency.)

Bazna got off scot-free. It was Ribbentrop and Kaltenbrunner who were to be executed. . . .

German spies in England weren't particularly successful in the Second World War. Not that they had been all that successful in the First World War either. There was no one to compare with Jules Silber; he was to remain unique. And his success is unlikely to be repeated because, as we have said elsewhere, the day of the freelance spy is over. Now spies must work in teams.

Colonel Oreste Pinto, known as the Spycatcher, wrote some very successful books and two successful TV series on his experiences as an interrogator of suspected German spies. He was also sent to see if he could trace Burgess and Maclean after the two Foreign Office spies disappeared, but he didn't get very far. Overall, though, the record of British counter-espionage was good. And the civilian population, alerted by cunning propaganda slogans – 'Careless talk costs lives' was a banner widely displayed on buses – were properly cautious.

There is a story that one young man suitably primed with false identity papers, who spoke immaculate English without the faintest trace of an accent, was caught because a neighbour in a village pub grew suspicious. Apparently the young man was keeping score during a darts match and he crossed a figure seven in the European way, although his story was that he had never been out of England. Inquiries into his background were made and discrepancies discovered.

Whether this story is true or not, spies *were* caught due to the vigilance of the British public.

It was left to Russian espionage to accomplish what the Germans couldn't; to penetrate into some of our most secret and highly guarded places. Let's look at some of the men and women who managed it.

5
The Atom Spy

The Americans spent vast sums of money on researching and developing the atom bomb; and it was one man, one man alone, who passed on the results of that research to the Russians. It's true that there were other atom spies working along similar lines, but there was only one Klaus Fuchs. The others were of secondary importance; it was Klaus Fuchs who saved his Soviet masters years of time and billions of roubles, because it was Klaus Fuchs who actually worked in the nerve centre of operations, and was highly qualified enough to explain to his opposite numbers exactly the right direction to take.

He was born in 1922 near Frankfurt, the son of a Quaker preacher (and hence a pacifist, as all Quakers are). The Nazis didn't like pacifists and Fuchs's father was sent to a concentration camp. His son managed to escape from Germany while that was still possible and came to England to stay with a cousin who was lodging with a Quaker family.

Young Klaus had another reason for wishing to escape the Nazis. At college in Germany he had been a prominent and very articulate member of the Communist Party. He was able to get a place at Bristol University to continue his studies in physics and mathematics; he hadn't been there very long before his tutors realized that here was a student of quite remarkable brilliance. In 1937 he finished his course and won a doctorate and a research scholarship to Edinburgh University.

He was, however, indiscreet enough to make no secret of his intense belief and faith in the cause of Marxism (Karl Marx was one of the founders of the communist doctrine, and is buried at Highgate Cemetery in London); the Chief Constable of Edinburgh warned the Home Office that this brilliant young German refugee who talked only about Russia really ought to be watched. But the Home Office had bigger fish to fry and no red tape stopped Klaus Fuchs from applying for British naturalization, which enables a foreigner to become a British subject.

But when war came in 1939, unavoidable delays occurred. Fuchs's request for naturalization didn't stop him from being interned, with a great many other refugees in Britain, on the Isle of Man. In 1940 he was moved across the Atlantic to an internment camp in Quebec, Canada.

Back in England, Fuchs's college professor, whose name was Max Born, was very angry at what he considered the high-handed action of the authorities. He argued that the country needed all the brains available, and that Fuchs ought to be freed at once and sent home.

Another important refugee scientist, Professor Rudolf Peierls, had become engaged in some important work at Birmingham University. He was trying to beat Germany in the race to build an atom bomb; Germany was thought to be two years ahead. Despite the fact that as early as 1918 it had been a Cambridge scientist, Ernest Rutherford, who had learned to split the atom, Britain had fallen behind in nuclear development, mainly through our constant bugbear, lack of funds. Peierls needed an expert in theoretical physics to complete his team and, with the help both of him and Max Born, Klaus Fuchs got the job.

It was while he was living with the professor and his family in Birmingham, and making frequent trips to London, that Fuchs first became a spy. It must have been on a strictly amateur basis, at least to start with; he didn't get much money out of it, probably not more than about £100 for ten years' work.

His legitimate work brought him more than adequate financial returns; he was highly qualified enough to demand a very substantial salary. We don't know whether he had any qualms about betraying his colleagues and those whose home he shared. Probably not: after all he became a spy not through greed but because he genuinely and passionately believed that the best future for all of us lay in the establishment of international communism.

It isn't clear how his first introduction to the KGB came about. It might have been through a member of the British Communist Party, or a friend at the Russian embassy, but it wasn't long before his name was added to the list of accredited Russian agents at the Moscow Centre. The man who was put in charge of him, his control, was Simon Kremer, secretary to the Soviet military attaché in London. Later Kremer was posted back to Moscow and a woman took over. She met Fuchs several times at Banbury, in Oxfordshire, and Moscow seemed quite satisfied with the regular details he supplied of his work on Peierls' atom bomb project.

At that stage the project itself was still considered comparatively small beer. It wasn't until 1943 that Peierls was ordered to go to Los Alamos, and of course he requested that Fuchs, his trusted assistant, should go with him. By that time Fuchs's naturalization papers were through and the American authorities saw no reason why he shouldn't be allowed in. Despite his Communist beliefs, neither British nor American security felt that they counted against him in any way, especially when placed against his scientific qualifications and usefulness. After all, the argument ran, most young men went through a leftish phase at university. This was of course true, but the fact remains that at the beginning of the war, as has been proved over and over again, security just wasn't tight enough.

America was extremely interested in nuclear research and felt that there wasn't a lot of sense in two political allies going about the same job independently. The Manhattan Project in Los Alamos, New Mexico, was more advanced in its work than the Birmingham University team and had far more money to play around with. There was every reason to pool ideas and with Fuchs' arrival in Los Alamos, they were pooled far more widely than even his bosses realized.

Another spy, David Greenglass, was already on the payroll. It was through him that Fuchs first met Yakovlev. Whether he met him in person or just through correspondence we don't know, but Fuchs had now definitely made the big time as a spy. Anatole Amanovich Yakovlev arrived in New York from Moscow in 1944 as the newly appointed Soviet vice-consul. He was about thirty-five and spoke fluent English, but his job as a diplomat was really a cover for something far more sinister. He was deputy director of the Second Directorate of the K G B – or rather its predecessor, which was known at that time as the N K V D.

Josef Stalin, leader of the U S S R, was anxious to establish a really efficient spy ring which would be based in New York. He had pretended firm and loyal friendship with America as a matter of expediency and had issued orders that the American Communist Party should be dissolved to show that he really wanted to be friends and an ally. But this surface attitude really fooled nobody.

Ostensibly it was Yakovlev's job to help to cement this shaky foundation, but in reality his task as one of the top espionage agents in Russia was to recruit and employ spies. What Stalin really wanted were the secrets of the Manhattan Project and Yakovlev came to the United States with a long list of potential traitors and 'sleeping' agents – those already recruited but with no assignments. At the top of the list were the names of Morris and Lona Cohen; we'll have much to say about them later, because they were to come to England and operate very successfully from a bungalow in Ruislip!

Under Yakovlev's control the spy ring grew rapidly. Also recruited were Julius and Ethel Rosenberg who were to die in the electric chair, Ethel's brother David Greenglass (a lathe operator in the Los Alamos atom-bomb plant), Harry Gold (a research chemist), and Morton Sobell, an electronics engineer working in the G E C Laboratories at Schenectady.

And of course Klaus Fuchs, who was already supplying information.

Among his most impressive reports, and one that really made Moscow sit up and take notice, was his account of the first atom-bomb test, which took place on 16 July 1945 at the air base just outside Alamagordo in the southern part of New Mexico. It was a dress rehearsal for the big ones, the bombs that destroyed Hiroshima and Nagasaki in Japan, three weeks later.

They frightened Japan into surrendering, but according to contemporary reports, Fuchs was appalled and depressed at the fury unleashed - as were so many other people. He had expected something big, but not something that could mean the end of the world. Harry Gold, the biochemist also recruited by Yakovlev, has said that at that time Fuchs, discussing how nuclear research could be applied for peaceful purposes, considered his career as a spy to be nearly over.

When the war ended in 1945, America and Britain decided that their scientists should not be allowed to work together in quite so free and easy a fashion and some parts of the Los Alamos plant were placed off limits to British personnel. Fuchs had asked to be permitted to visit the United States plutonium plant at Hanford in Washington, but his request had been turned down. So it came about that in 1946 he was ordered back to England and went to work on theoretical physics at the newly opened Atomic Energy Establishment near Harwell in Berkshire.

Moscow still required his services, and it wasn't long before he was instructed to present himself at 8 p.m. on the first Saturday in every month outside the station at Teddington in Middlesex. To make sure that he was recognized, he was to carry five books tied together with a piece of string. He was even told that the bundle should be supported by two fingers of his right hand! A spy's directions are nothing if not precise!

There were other arranged meetings at pubs: the Nag's

Head at Wood Green, north London, and the Spotted Horse in Putney. On these occasions Fuchs carried a copy of the left-wing weekly, *Tribune*. His opposite number held a book bound in red. Apparently Fuchs didn't turn up for every meeting; perhaps by that time his prestige as an information source was such that Moscow allowed him some leeway.

In 1949 a tip-off came from the FBI that there might be more to Klaus Fuchs than met the eye. The head of security at Harwell contacted William Skardon, a top MI5 interrogator who began looking into the background of this strange individual who worked so industriously and lived so simply. Klaus was given promotion and a salary increase so that his suspicions wouldn't be aroused; Skardon began making trips to the Fuchs's bungalow and the talks he had both there and at Harwell finally convinced him that Fuchs was his man.

Klaus Fuchs was arrested by George Smith at the Ministry of Supply, to which he'd gone to attend what he believed to be a routine conference. (It must have looked like something out of 'This is Your Life', with the Special Branch substituting for Eamonn Andrews!) On 1 March 1950 he was sentenced to fourteen years in jail. His defence, that he only wanted to share with Russia information that would help her to win against Germany, cut no ice.

On his release, Klaus Fuchs went to East Germany, where he now holds an important academic post.

He was finally induced to confess by William Skardon, who was later given the job of questioning Kim Philby, the Foreign Office mole. Skardon wasn't so successful with Philby, who was able to get away and defect to Moscow.

There was no doubt that Klaus Fuchs and his information paved the way for the Russians' own atom bomb, which they produced in 1949. The shock to Anglo-American relations was very great and wasn't helped by the revelations about Soviet infiltration into the British Foreign Office. Fuchs gave the Russians hard scientific facts: not only about the atomic bomb but also about the even more powerful hydrogen bomb. He knew practically everything there was to know about these weapons, their sizes, what they contained, how they were built and detonated. After his exposure – and also those of Dr Nunn May (who got ten years) and a Dr Bruno Pontecorvo (who defected just in time), both of whom were involved in other areas of nuclear research – screening by the security service was tightened up considerably.

When he had been working at Los Alamos, Fuchs's contact for part of the time had been an agent known as Raymonde. The FBI had their suspicions as to who Raymonde was, but they weren't sure. Their enquiries led to Harry Gold, the research chemist. Could Gold be Raymonde?

Gold worked at the Philadelphia General Hospital, and as was later proved, was one of Yakovlev's recruits. He had already been the subject of a security check when the FBI were working on another case, but they were still keeping an eye on him. When they went to see him in connection with the Fuchs case, Gold told them that he had never travelled west of the Mississippi. But he was trapped by his own lie when they found a town plan of Santa Fe on his bookcase.

How was the name of Klaus Fuchs brought forward in the first place? Not through any slip of his own. It was through the kind of thing which always has been, and always will continue to be, an occupational hazard in the life of an espionage agent . . . and one against which he had little defence.

Klaus Fuchs was given away by a Soviet defector.

6
Cold War Spies

Defectors don't always speak the truth. In Britain, their evidence isn't valid in a court of law and has to be supported by proof. The reason for this is obvious, if you stop to think about it. A defector usually feels pretty passionately about what he is doing, and equally passionately about wanting to convince those to whom he is running that he's worth their attention. So the temptation to manufacture false evidence must be high.

Colonel Anatole Golitzin, who defected to America in 1961, gave the CIA evidence that led to the suspicion that former Leader of the Opposition in the British House of Commons, Hugh Gaitskell, who died of an obscure disease, had in fact been assassinated by the KGB. The motive apparently was to get rid of a future Labour prime minister who was far too anti-Communist for the Kremlin's taste. Despite the fact that the KGB is not averse to a spot of murder on the side, nobody really believed this and his family were able to produce proof that it was nonsense. Another defector claimed that Harold Wilson was really a Soviet agent, still another that the famous Great Train Robbery was organized by British Intelligence to get extra funds.

It's tempting in the face of these wild allegations to dismiss what defectors tell us out of hand. This would be a very dangerous thing to do, because over and over again lists of spies delivered by defectors have been proved by subsequent investigations to be only too accurate. In many cases master spies and spymasters, intelligent enough not to make their own mistakes, would *never* have been caught had it not been for evidence from the side to which they've sold their information.

Occasionally spies have been caught by accident. This happened in the case of a Soviet spy operating in the United States.

A highway patrol car was receiving strange atmospheric effects on its radio. The police officers at first thought little of this, but since this strange, shrill sound occurred frequently and was not received on other patrol car radios, they decided to have their radio checked.

The radio repairman could find nothing wrong and gave his considered opinion that the whistling they got was a form of transmission. But short of aliens from outer space, who would want to transmit unintelligible sounds? The only explanation seemed to be that they were high-frequency coded messages.

The FBI were consulted, and the strange transmissions recorded. Code experts worked on the recording, and reported that indeed high-frequency messages were being transmitted, but the code used was indecipherable. The next job was to find out where the transmissions were coming from. The FBI began following the patrol car on its duty tours and observed that transmissions were stronger near the main highway. After some days, they noticed that whenever the transmission started up, a blue

Chevrolet was parked somewhere along the highway. If there were no transmissions, there was no Chevrolet.

When the FBI agents approached the Chevrolet, the occupant lost his nerve, pulled a gun and tried to shoot himself out. His car was found to be equipped with a powerful miniature transmitter which by a weird coincidence happened to be tuned to broadcast on the same wavelength as the one used by the radio of the highway patrol car radio.

But normally it's defectors rather than car radios that catch spies. Igor Gouzenko was a young cable clerk working at the Soviet embassy in Ottawa under Colonel Nikolai Zabotin, the Russian military attaché, who was really a spymaster operating a network of spies throughout Canada. One day young Igor was ordered to return to Russia; but he and his wife Anna had decided they preferred the West and as proof of his wish to become a useful Canadian citizen, he went to the embassy safe and took out all the most secret and damaging documents he could lay his hands on. This was in September 1945 and to this day all the names on that list haven't been published.

We've pointed out that the defector isn't a recent phenomenon. There have been defectors as long as there have been spies. But it has only been in the uneasy days of the Cold War between East and West that informers have really won such devastating power.

The atmosphere of a cold war is conducive to espionage: it is a 'climate of treason', as Andrew Boyle called it in the book that first exposed Anthony Blunt as a spy. In a 'hot' war, hostility is declared openly and we know where we are. But in a 'cold' war it all goes on under the surface. Distrust and secrecy flourish, breeding more distrust and secrecy.

Ever since the end of the Second World War this state of Cold War has existed. The term was first coined by Winston Churchill, and like so much that was said by this master of language, it expressed the situation perfectly.

Whether Klaus Fuchs's name was on Gouzenko's list we don't know for sure. There was certainly a nice little gift-wrapped box of atom spies, and someone who was mentioned was Dr Alan Nunn May, a lecturer in physics at King's College, London, who was previously at Cambridge with the Foreign Office spies, Burgess, Maclean, Philby and Blunt.

Dr Nunn May worked on secret nuclear research, particularly in the production and use of refined uranium, at the Canadian Government's plant at Chalk River; under the codename, Alek, he had been passing information to Lieutenant Angelov, assistant military attaché at the Soviet embassy. The information included details about the methods and materials used.

Another name on Gouzenko's file was that of the Italian Dr Bruno Pontecorvo, who worked at the Harwell Atomic Energy Establishment, and who defected to Russia before he could be arrested.

Now the KGB had to rebuild the structure destroyed by Gouzenko and in 1948 they sent one of their best men over to New York. His name was Rudolph Abel and, like Gordon Lonsdale, he was a KGB colonel.

As Emil R. Golfus he settled in Brooklyn, and was known as an artist who dabbled in photography. He also played the guitar and, as a kind of double bluff, let it be known that he was an amateur radio enthusiast. His neighbours, of course, were not in the picture as to how enthusiastic he really was! Under this cover he built up a network concerned mainly with sending information on nuclear weapons and rocketry to Moscow.

He was arrested through no fault of his own. How often we have to say this about professional spies! His particular Achilles heel was a communications officer named Reino Hayhanen, a member of the Russian security police who was also an alcoholic with a grievance!

Hayhanen was a reluctant spy. He didn't want to be a spy at all, but had hoped for the quiet, safe job of a chauffeur in a foreign embassy. Instead he was sent as Abel's assistant. Abel didn't trust him and eventually arranged for him to be recalled. Frightened of what might happen to him when he returned to Moscow, Hayhanen defected.

He did this from Paris, having sailed from New York, his orders being to contact a Soviet agent in Paris who was to arrange his trip home.

This is what happened next. On 26 April 1957 a man came to the United States embassy in Paris demanding to see the ambassador. At first the officials thought he was a crank, but when he began to talk of a large spy ring, mentioning names and places, he was taken to a security official. The visitor then took a five-cent coin from his pocket, pressed its rim between his fingers and opened it. It was hollow and in the cavity was a tiny piece of microfilm.

The official was stunned. It reminded him of an earlier incident which had puzzled the FBI for several years. In 1953 a newspaper boy, fourteen-year-old James Bozart, had come to a New York police precinct carrying a coin that had been given to him as payment for a newspaper. This five-cent piece had slipped from his fingers and when he bent to pick it up he saw that it had been split into two halves.

Inside one was a minute strip of film. The boy must have read some spy thrillers and he took the nickel to the police.

They didn't know what to make of it, and it was passed to the FBI. After the microfilm was enlarged it was found to show the picture of a card, possibly an index card, with several rows of numbers, undoubtedly a cipher key. The CIA tried to solve the puzzle, while the FBI tried to trace the man who had bought the newspaper from James Bozart and had given him the coin, obviously in error. He was never found but the cryptanalysts solved the code. It was based on a Russian folk song and its basic key was the Russian word for 'snowfall'.

There was hardly a doubt that the coin was part of a spy's equipment, but the split nickel and its contents remained a mystery until the strange visitor produced a similar one in Paris.

He was Reino Hayhanen of the KGB and chief assistant to Rudolph Abel.

He talked and Abel was arrested. For nine years, since 1948, Abel had been a successful operator. His misgivings about Hayhanen had proved well founded.

The road that had brought Abel to Brooklyn had been a long one. Born in Russia in 1902, he became a teacher in a spy school run by OGPU, the KGB forerunner. In 1945 he was parachuted into Germany as a secret agent.

When he arrived in the United States in 1948 he had just the right gifts to make an ideal spy. He was not only an expert operator of shortwave radio sets, he could also repair them. He was an expert in micro-photography, from the preparation of tiny reproductions of maps to the preparing of microdot copies of secret reports. His skill as a metal craftsman made it easy for him to hollow out screws and cufflinks, and this is how he sent bits of film out. It was probably his idea to hollow out the coin.

Perhaps that was the key to his brilliance: he was good with small things. Each of his agents knew him by a different name and each had his own code; all were devised by Abel. The location of every dead-letter drop used by the network was printed on the map of his mind. One was concealed on a park bench, another in the toilet of a Brooklyn bar. . . .

His first setback occurred in February 1950 when Klaus Fuchs was arrested. When Fuchs was finally induced to talk, he went on talking. Harry Gold, David Greenglass, the Rosenbergs and several other members of the ring were rounded up. Yakovlev hurriedly returned to Moscow.

Abel didn't panic, though. He lay low for a time, his radio set remaining silent for a year.

In 1951 he was back in business and it was through a radio transmission direct from Moscow that he heard about Hayhanen's betrayal. He fled to Florida and enjoyed the sunshine undisturbed for some weeks. Then he came back and booked in at a hotel under the name of Martin Collins.

That was where they caught up with him. He was arrested and went on trial in New York in October 1957. His lawyer, James Donovan, skilfully fought off the prosecution, which demanded the death penalty.

'Who knows,' Donovan said, 'but that at some later date an American might not fall into Russian hands charged with similar offences. If Colonel Abel is then still alive, maybe it will be possible to effect an exchange of prisoners.'

The judge gave Abel thirty years instead of sentencing him to death.

Donovan was right. Nearly three years later, an American

named Francis Gary Powers literally fell into Russian hands from out of the sky!

One final incident occurred. Reino Hayhanen, the self-confessed spy, was never prosecuted. After Abel's conviction he stayed in the United States under the protection of the CIA and with a new alias. Apparently he worked for the CIA until 1961 when he made his first appearance on TV, commenting on the spy trials of the Portland spy ring in Britain. Wearing dark glasses, hair and moustache dyed auburn, his appearance had changed very considerably. Nevertheless, shortly after his TV appearance he was dead, killed in a mysterious car crash on the Pennsylvania Turnpike. The other car didn't stop.

Francis Gary Powers was an American air force pilot. He was also the son of a Kentucky coalminer who after a pit accident had turned to shoe-repairing. In 1950, aged twenty-one, Gary Powers was drafted into the US air force. He qualified as a pilot two years later and was given the rank of lieutenant.

He was an outstanding pilot, so much so that three years later he was approached by a superior officer and asked whether he would consider a new form of flying. It would mean serving for at least eighteen months overseas, but the pay would be very much better than that of a USAF fighter pilot.

He was told that his employers would be the CIA, though nobody must know this. The penalty for breaking the Secrets Act would be $10,000. He was told that ostensibly he would be doing weather reconnaissance, that the United States had secured two bases near the Soviet border, one in Turkey, the other in Pakistan.

All he had to do was to fly a U2 plane up and down this border. Instruments inside the plane would record information about Russian radar and radio installations. He would use the name Palmer as a cover, and as Palmer he would be given identity documents.

He was also given something far more sinister: it was a silver dollar, but this coin wouldn't contain microfilm. Inside was a lethal poison, the same kind of thing that was issued to Resistance saboteurs and agents during the Second World War. He could take it or not, at his discretion, if he were captured, tortured and the pain proved too much. When his plane did crash, he threw it away, preferring to take his chance among the living.

After two and a half months of training, Powers was posted to Peshawar in Pakistan, the second of the two US bases. One day his commanding officer told him he had been chosen for a very special mission. Up to now he had never ventured more than a mile or two inside Soviet territory, but now he was to cross Afghanistan, making a one-way flight to Bodo in Norway, where he would eventually land. This meant that the young pilot was to fly right across Russia – quite a test for Powers and the U2, and the first solo attempt.

This flight marked the climax of a series of shorter 'weather reconnaissance' forays flown by Powers and the other U2 pilots, which produced hundreds of miles of film and a really comprehensive picture of the Soviet Union from a height of thirteen miles.

Just what was so special about the U2?

As we saw earlier, the Spitfire had been developed for what came to be known as aerial reconnaissance by a resourceful man called Sydney Cotton, who with his team carried out certain modifications. By removing the Spitfires' guns, and making changes to the engines, their speed could be increased from 360 m.p.h. to 400 m.p.h., their altitude to 30,000 feet and their range to 1250 miles. This added up to aircraft that could fly higher and faster than anything owned by the German Air Force. Painted light blue to blend with the sky, the Spitfire XIX was an early link in the chain that would eventually produce spy satellites.

The British were the first to initiate special spy flights after the Second World War and in 1953 RAF Canberra bombers flew with cameras over sites in west Kazakhastan, where the Soviets were suspected of testing long-range missiles. But the photographs were fuzzy and not much use.

As happens so often in the history of British enterprise, money for research ran out and the Americans took over. President Eisenhower told aviation experts to design an aircraft with every speed possible, money no object, that would be able to 'fly above the range of all known rockets and interceptors'.

Draughtsmen and engineers were sworn to secrecy and worked flat out. Nine months later the prototype was in the air and the Utility 2 was born. Up to the time Powers embarked on his fateful mission, its record had been excellent.

He marked the route on his map; little red and blue markings denoted where he had to press the knobs that activated the cameras and recording devices. He was approaching the outskirts of Sverdlovsk when it happened. As he said later, 'I saw it, that is – I felt a sort of hollow-sounding explosion. It seemed to be behind me. I could see an orange flash.'

The U2 suddenly went out of control. All sorts of things began to go wrong. His legs were wedged under the instrument panel so the ejector wasn't safe to use. The force would have torn them from his body. He had no time to operate the device that would have destroyed the plane in mid-air, thus preventing the espionage equipment from falling into Soviet hands: by the time he got his legs free and had grabbed his parachute, it was too late. He was falling out of the plane and the U2 was still intact.

The result of all this was an international incident that hit the headlines all over the world. The wreck of the crashed plane, damning evidence of espionage, was placed on public exhibition in Moscow and Gary Powers found himself in Lublanka Prison.

He was sentenced to ten years' imprisonment, but after only seventeen months he was exchanged for Rudolph Abel.

Colonel Abel returned to the shadows. He did, however, express his gratitude to James Donovan by sending him two rare and valuable books. He remembered that Donovan was a collector.

Gary Powers was later awarded the Intelligence Star of the CIA, the highest decoration given to American secret agents. In 1970 he published his memoirs.

The Russian leaders chose to publicize the incident of Gary Powers and the U2 for their own purposes. But it was only a minor setback for the spy planes. Their contribution to aerial reconnaissance is incalculable; it was largely evidence from U2 photographs that enabled President Kennedy to discover that the Russians were building missile bases in Cuba, uncomfortably near North America. The nearest the West has ever come to World War Three, the crisis was averted when Khrushchev had his bluff called, and agreed to stop their construction.

The Lublanka Prison has been the temporary home of many spies. After his arrest in 1962, Greville Wynne was taken there before he was exchanged for Gordon Lonsdale, whom we'll look at more closely in a later chapter.

Wynne was first recruited into the intelligence services in 1938, when he was an engineering apprentice at University College, Nottingham, and working in a local factory. One evening he returned to the factory to collect some books and heard a man apparently transmitting radio messages to Germany. It was as a result of reporting this incident that he was recruited.

He spent the war in 'low-level counter-intelligence', as he called it. He didn't much like it, but was given rather more interesting missions later, when he was able to cloak his espionage activities beneath legitimate business interests; he had started as a sales representative for an engineering company but later began his own export business, Mobile Exhibitions Ltd, which represented British industrial and commercial firms abroad.

As an agent he worked very closely with yet another KGB colonel, Oleg Penkovsky, who had been persuaded to turn traitor because he loathed Khrushchev. Before he was arrested, at the same time as Wynne, and shot, Penkovsky had given to Britain a great deal of valuable information. On his visits to this country he was given the red-carpet treatment and once even attended a royal garden party!

In his book *The Man from Odessa,* Wynne tells us all about his first postwar assignment.

His job was to assist in the escape from the USSR of

Major Sergei Kuznov, an associate of Penkovsky's and like him a Soviet intelligence officer who had been spying for the British.

The escape plan had been devised by Kuznov himself, and Wynne's part was fairly dangerous. He was to go to Moscow and ask the Intourist travel agency to book him on a cruise to see the sights, arranging that he would join the ship at Odessa.

Wynne's contact told him that after he boarded the ship at Odessa, while she was still tied up at the dock, he would have to have an accident. A side rail on one of the docks would give way and Wynne would have to fall over onto the quayside below.

'Don't worry,' his contact said, 'the drop won't be more than twenty feet and you're going to land on a pile of sand that cushions your fall. Cry out loudly when you hit the ground. We expect the searchlights will swing over to give you assistance. That's the whole point of the operation. While everyone's attending to you, the major is going to slip out in a small boat from another part of the harbour and transfer to a foreign merchantman that's just getting under way at the moment you make your fall. Timing is, of course, essential.'

It was planned that Wynne would meet Kuznov in a hotel in Odessa a few days before the boat sailed. He had some money to give him 'to pay off those who have helped arrange the escape'. The money was disguised inside a packet of Russian cigarettes. When the two came into contact as arranged, Kuznov had something for Wynne in return: a message proposing that they meet the following day at a football stadium.

While a football game was in progress and with the crowd

roaring all round them, the major slipped an envelope into
Wynne's pocket. He spoke quickly and quietly under cover
of the noise. 'I'm going to tell you what's in that envelope,'
he said. 'It outlines a plan to build a wall between the
eastern and western zones of Berlin.'

The idea seemed preposterous to Wynne but he agreed to
deliver the envelope. One thing bothered him though. It
would be on him when he had to take the tumble; he
couldn't risk having his luggage searched. What did the
major suggest?

Luckly the major knew the cruise boat. 'There are
lavatories outside the entrance to the bar,' he said. 'Hide
the envelope in one of the ventilation ducts. The grille
comes off easily. It's held in place with self-tapping screws.
You'll find some tape in the package. Use that to stick it to
the inside of the ducts.'

The ship was due to lift anchor at half past midnight.
Wynne got on board just after nine and hid the envelope as
planned. So far so good. Now time for a drink.

At 11.30 I left the bar and strolled along the deck. I found the
spot where the bulkhead light was out of commission and ran my
hand along the railing until I came to a section that wiggled like a
loose tooth. Who had seen to these arrangements? I did not know.

I was very conscious as the seconds ticked by that I had to look
out to sea and identify the foreign ship moving slowly out of the
harbour so that I could synchronize my leap. It had been worked
out in London that I was to jump as soon as the merchantman's
bow was directly in line with the cruise ship's single funnel.

Wynne swallowed hard and launched himself over the side.
The concussion of impact seemed to shatter him into a
million pieces. . . .

There was no sand!

Wynne was to hear later that the intelligence department had slipped up. In hospital he was told that he would have to undergo an operation for a fractured hip and that it would take at least three months to get him back on his feet again.

It all seemed to have gone hopelessly wrong. He had to get out of the Soviet Union as fast as possible for the plan to succeed, and he had no way of knowing what had happened to Kuznov.

He told the doctors that a stay of three months would be disastrous for his business. Eventually the doctors were prevailed upon to agree to strap him up in plaster like a mummy and fly him back to London. But he would have to get to Moscow first.

He caught a BEA flight but it all meant that the cruise left Odessa without him. And the package was still hidden in the loo!

Back in London, his contact came to visit him in St George's Hospital. He told him that the sand had been correctly positioned on the day that Wynne was supposed to make his fall, but that it had been raining and somebody had come along and placed a tarpaulin over the sand to protect it. So what Wynne had landed on was the tarpaulin, although it had felt like concrete.

He was requested to finish the job he had started, so three months later he found himself on a flight to Bulgaria to meet the ship which was due to tie up at a Bulgarian port. He got a visitor's pass, went on board and found the duty officer, who remembered both him and the accident.

'They found the railings were not correctly fixed,' the officer said, 'and the broken lamp had not been replaced as it should have been. The verdict was accident.'

Wynne says that the officer was a little surprised to see him, but he made the excuse that he wanted to thank the officer personally for his kindness in looking after him and arranging the ambulance. The officer seemed satisfied with this and then Wynne asked him to have a drink. While they were waiting in the bar, he slipped out to the loo.

I was the only occupant. My luck was still holding; I had not forgotten my pocket screwdriver, and quickly turned the screws to undo the grille.

It pulled loose. Without pausing I reached into the shaft and felt my heart leap as my fingers brushed against the package. Three cheers for Russian adhesive tape! I could still hardly bring myself to believe my luck. I pulled the envelope loose, and stuffed it hastily in my pocket. Then I replaced the grille, and went back to the bar.

So the plans for the Berlin Wall, with Khrushchev's own signature on the photostat, had been locked in a ship's loo for three months!

When Penkovsky and Wynne were arrested in Moscow, Wynne escaped with his life, and eventual freedom through a spy exchange. Penkovsky wasn't so lucky.

Another spy whom death claimed was the frogman Lionel 'Buster' Crabbe. The circumstances surrounding that death still haven't been cleared up completely.

In the early fifties it had become standard practice for navies to indulge in underwater intelligence operations against warships of potential enemies. Nowhere was this more blatantly true than in the harbour of Leningrad. British ships on goodwill missions had their hulls exam-ined by Russian frogmen who wanted to know their fighting capacities or any other details they could prise out. The British protested but their complaints were ignored.

The Russian cruiser *Sverdlov* came to Portsmouth in 1953 to take part in the Queen's coronation celebrations. Naval frogmen who wanted to have a tit-for-tat look at the opposition were forbidden by the authorities from doing so: they were told, 'The coronation is not a proper occasion for such activities.'

The *Sverdlov* was back in Portsmouth in 1955, this time on a naval goodwill visit, and this time MI6 decided to go ahead.

Crabbe, known to his friends as Buster after the Hollywood actor who had played Flash Gordon in the thirties' serials, had won the George medal for wartime underwater operations in the Mediterranean, particularly in Gibraltar where he had removed limpet mines from British ships as fast as Italian frogmen could attach them. He was a freelance recently retired from the Navy, and he was carefully informed that if anything went wrong the Admiralty, which was in charge of the protection of all Russian ships in British harbours, would deny all knowledge of what was going on. With that proviso he was given the go-ahead to find out what he could about the ship by examining every inch of her structure.

Naval intelligence was delighted with the results – the mission was a success.

Eight months later, Khrushchev and Bulganin, the joint heads of the Soviet Union, were due in Britain for a visit and, whether it was MI6 or Crabbe himself who made the decision, a return visit was organized.

On 17 April Crabbe and an MI6 officer checked into a small Portsmouth hotel; the next day Crabbe entered the water with the gear he needed for a session of surreptitious underwater photography.

At 7.30 he was seen by some Russian sailors swimming on the surface near a Russian destroyer. He was having difficulty in getting down deep enough and had decided to return for an extra pound of ballast weight. He didn't realize he had been seen.

After a discussion with the MI6 officer, he decided to take a break and return for the final inspection in the afternoon. He made a phone call to London and was seen in a pub at 2 p.m.

He made that final dive but he never returned alive. MI6 believes that he died accidentally either through oxygen poisoning – damage to his oxygen supply-line – or through diving too deep under the cruiser's hull. Later a detective visited the Portsmouth hotel and removed from the hotel register all evidence that he'd ever stayed there.

Despite the fact that Russian intelligence agents had been doing similar underwater reconnaissance for years, Bulganin and Khrushchev decided to make political capital out of the Crabbe incident and stormed around full of righteous indignation. The Prime Minister at the time, Anthony Eden, was forced to answer questions in Parliament and had to claim that 'whatever was done was done without the authority or the knowledge of ministers' and that 'disciplinary action had been taken'.

The Russian sailors reported seeing a frogman, and everyone agreed that it was Crabbe.

Fourteen months later, in June 1957, a frogman's headless body was washed up near Chichester harbour. What was left of the suit was identical with the one worn by Crabbe, and the coroner's verdict was that it was Crabbe.

So what had happened? Had the Russians murdered him? The fact that his head had disappeared gave rise to all sorts of rumours. One theory was that rival frogmen had been lying in wait and had ambushed him. A headless body was then dressed in his suit and dumped from a Russian submarine to fool British intelligence. Perhaps Crabbe was alive and, if not exactly well, at least living in Moscow.

But it later transpired that a body with head attached had been dredged up by a lone fisherman a few months before. He had grabbed the head to haul it in and it had come away in his hands. He dropped the whole grisly relic in horror and went to tell the local police, but they took no action beyond filing a report. Perhaps they didn't believe him.

Even after the inquest the Admiralty refused to admit that Crabbe had been spying. The official story, which they were sticking to, was that he was making a 'test dive in connection with the trials of certain underwater apparatus' at Stokes Bay, three miles from Portsmouth.

Whatever the truth surrounding Crabbe's death, the sea can claim another unsolved mystery. It's probably true that Crabbe died through 'misadventure', the coroner's verdict. As journalist Chapman Pincher says, he was forty-six, drinking and smoking heavily, and not really fit for this *Boys' Own Paper* stuff. He had been seen in a pub just before the dive.

In the next chapter we'll look at some more naval spies.

7
Naval Spies

The first that the British public heard about what came to be known as the Portland spy ring was news of the discovery of some strange equipment in a bungalow in the Home Counties suburb of Ruislip.

The police had come to visit the bungalow because they wanted to talk to the couple who owned it, who were living under the name of Kroger. They were friends of Gordon Lonsdale; and Lonsdale, together with two of his accomplices, Harry Houghton and Ethel Gee, had already been arrested at Waterloo Station in a highly organized Special Branch operation. The police had been following them for some days and a shopping basket containing Admiralty secrets had changed hands at the station in full view of the watching officers.

But much as he already knew, Superintendent George Smith who was in charge of the case didn't know about the Ruislip bungalow. He didn't know that it would prove to be the centre of the whole spy ring.

There isn't space here to describe everything that was uncovered; we'll just look at a few of the more important bits of equipment.

The first thing detectives examined was a Ronson table lighter. Its wooden base had been hollowed out, and from this hiding place detectives took signal plans covering transmission times and frequencies over a period of eight months, one of them with headings in Russian, and pads used to put messages into code.

Other small items proved to be not what they appeared. Then Smith turned his attention to the radiogram, taking up most of one wall of the sitting room. At the back of it he found a pair of headphones and loose flex. In the bedroom he discovered a microscope and five glass slides. Under a chest of drawers, wrapped in a blue bathing costume, was a 35 mm film magazine and 49 feet of electric flex with a bulb at one end and a plug at the other. From the ricepaper pages of a Bible in a bookcase came a white-coated piece of cellophane, which was used by Russian agents to make microdot photographs. A whisky flask on a bedside table contained three compartments, in one of which was a black powder also used for microdot printing. A torch in the same drawer had a secret cavity. In the bathroom a tin of talcum powder contained a microdot reader.

But it was when the detectives got to the kitchen that the fun really started. In the floor was a trap door giving access to a cellar and in the cellar, hidden under a pile of rubble, they found a grey, metal box. This box contained a radio transmitter powerful enough to send messages direct to Moscow. Beside the box they found another false torch, lenses used to make microdots and a camera and photographic equipment. There was also a keying device that enabled them to send long messages in a very short time, and a considerable amount of money.

The loft of the bungalow contained a radio aerial which

was much too long for a normal set: at 74 feet, it was powerful enough for the Krogers to pick up instructions from Moscow on their apparently innocent radiogram.

More photographic equipment was found in the bathroom, far more sophisticated and specialized than even the most enthusiastic amateur would need – and the Krogers had never convinced their neighbours that they had even a passing interest in photography, apart from the normal taking of holiday snaps. As well as 35 mm cameras, a lens system was found which made it obvious that the majority of the documents stolen from the Portland naval base were photographed and the 35 mm negatives reduced to microdots little larger than a full stop on a printed page. They could be inserted in an apparently innocent letter, sealed behind the stamp on an envelope – or sent out of the country in a book.

It was this last method that Kroger adopted. His book-selling business, for which he had customers in many parts of the world, made it natural for him to send parcels abroad. He was such a regular caller at Ruislip Post Office that at Christmas he took the girls chocolates.

The books he sent out concealed other books, complete miniatures concealed in microdots stuck onto the text, or in the binding. Often the addresses where he sent his parcels were mere collection points, post-office boxes or whatever; the Russian agents who collected them would then repack and re-address them to their final destinations in Russia. He would send coded radio messages from the bungalow, telling Moscow Centre that the books were on their way and where they could be picked up.

To anyone not in the know, the Krogers sold antiquarian and rare books, and there was no doubt that they did know quite a lot about books. They had premises in the Strand, London, and were really quite successful.

Perhaps it's now time to reveal the truth about the Krogers. When Colonel Rudolph Abel was arrested in New York, photographs of a couple called the Cohens were discovered in his hotel room. The Cohens and the Krogers were one and the same.

Colonel Abel himself obviously knew something about rare books, judging from the present he sent his lawyer James Donovan after he had negotiated his release from prison in exchange for Gary Powers, the U2 pilot. I wonder if it is too far-fetched to establish a link here: perhaps the Cohens and Abel had talked about books at some time and the Cohens had communicated something of their own enthusiasm to their spymaster.

The FBI had sent the Cohens' fingerprints to Britain when they were searching for them in New York after Abel was arrested. Nobody was more surprised than the detectives at Scotland Yard's Criminal Records Office when they found many months later that the prints checked with those of the Krogers!

Morris Cohen was born in the Bronx, a tough multiracial district of New York, in 1911, the elder son of a Jewish grocer who had been born in Russia. Lona Cohen was born in Massachusetts but her family came from Poland. It was while Morris was studying for a Master of Arts degree in social studies at Illinois University that he first became a communist sympathizer. When the Abraham Lincoln Brigade was raised in America to fight against Franco in the Spanish Civil War, Cohen joined. Later he became a school-master and in 1942 went to work for the Russians – legitimately, as it happened. He was with AMTORG, an organization which was involved in trade between the Soviet Union and the United States at a time when the two countries were firmly united allies; though AMTORG was officially recognized, it could have been the means by which he was first recruited. It was certainly around this time that the Cohens first met the Rosenbergs and Colonel Abel, who was running his successful New York spy ring.

When that broke up in 1950, Morris Cohen put it about that he had been offered a job as a Hollywood scriptwriter. But it was in England that he eventually surfaced.

We've already seen that many major spy cases are connected, like links in a chain. When Igor Gouzenko, the cipher clerk in the Russian embassy in Ottawa, decided in 1945 that he wanted to stay in the West, he brought with him documents in which the name of Allan Nunn May, the British atomic scientist, appeared. When Nunn May was arrested, a name scribbled on an envelope found in his home was ignored. This name was that of Dr Klaus Fuchs. As we have seen, Fuchs's contact while he was working in Los Alamos had been Harry Gold. Gold led the police to David Greenglass, who was the brother of Ethel Rosenberg. It was the Rosenbergs who recruited the Cohens.

We don't know where they went for the five years in which they were hiding out. Did they meet Gordon Lonsdale then?

What *is* known is that he arrived in England just two months after the Cohen–Krogers, and he came via Canada.

To this day nobody in the West is absolutely certain what his real name was. (Or is, because as far as we know he is still alive.) It might have been Konon Trofimovich Molody. But what *is* certain is that he masterminded the whole Portland operation.

His early life is shrouded in mystery (as is his later). In his memoirs he claims to have worked in the Polish Resistance against the Nazis and to have first met Colonel Abel when the latter had infiltrated the German army before the war. According to this same book, Abel had joined the Abwehr, German intelligence, and one of his jobs was to interrogate Russian prisoners.

The memoirs were proved pretty conclusively to be nothing more than Russian propaganda, and must be taken with a hefty pinch of salt. As must Lonsdale's boast, made after his release from prison and return to Moscow in 1964, that 'For five years I stole American atom secrets.' He claimed that he did this while living in a New York apartment near Central Park, assisting Rudolph Abel and working with many other Soviet agents, some employed by the United Nations.

There's no documentary proof that Lonsdale was actually a member of Abel's spy ring. What *is* certain is that he was recruited into the KGB after the Second World War and that when he stole passports and papers from the real Gordon Lonsdale, he had already achieved the rank of colonel.

When he got to England in 1954, the colonel set about the task of establishing a front and this he did with practised ease. Actually, of all unlikely occupations he set himself up as a juke box salesman, and in 1955 began trading in bubble gum machines! He went into partnership with a man called Peter Ayres, who was planning to launch a company at Broadstairs on the Kent coast.

Lonsdale's energy was incredible. He was learning Chinese at the School of Oriental Studies, hawking bubble gum machines and establishing contacts in his legitimate business, entertaining hordes of girlfriends and all the while establishing and maintaining his spy network.

He had a flat in a luxury block in London called the White House; from here he transmitted and received radio messages from Moscow much as the Krogers did. He had to make frequent furtive visits to the dead-letter boxes where other agents deposited snippets of information that formed a vital part of the intelligence system, and he had to ensure that he always had an adequate supply of cash available to distribute as wages.

He had to make trips to Ruislip and he had to recruit new agents. Two of these were Harry Houghton and Ethel Gee, but when Gordon Lonsdale brought Harry Houghton into the organization he made his first, and last, big mistake.

Before we look at Mr Houghton, let's look at what the Portland spy ring was.

It was all about underwater detection. Russia was realizing that the NATO countries were beginning to take the lead in developing new techniques for underwater detection and Soviet naval chiefs badly wanted to know how far ahead they were.

ASDICS are devices which record echoes if transmitted soundwaves strike an undersea object and their main purpose is for detecting enemy submarines. At that time the ones in use had certain drawbacks: they were accurate only over comparatively short distances, and even within those limits rough weather could throw them out. German U-Boat commanders had discovered that temperature changes could 'bend' the transmitted soundwaves, making it impossible to take an exact fix on a submarine's position from a boat on the surface. New ASDICS that worked far more efficiently were being developed, but they worked on different principles and the Russians wanted to know what those principles were. They also wanted to know the areas where these new inventions were to be tried out, and the results of those trials.

This was the main information that the Portland spy ring wanted. Lonsdale and the Krogers were highly professional espionage agents and it was unfortunate for them that they couldn't manage without employing the services of amateurs. Harry Houghton and Ethel Gee were in a position to be able to get hold of the secrets Russia wanted; their sole motivation was greed.

Harry Houghton worked as a clerk in the Underwater Weapons Establishment and so did his mistress Ethel Gee. Houghton was already known to the Russians, as this former naval master-at-arms had worked from July 1951 to October 1952 as a naval attaché's writer (clerk) at the British embassy in Warsaw. A full dossier is kept automatically on those in junior, lower-paid posts in foreign embassies, because it is often among them that the Russians feel they have the best chance of finding recruits. Houghton was considered a good choice because he had a weakness: drink.

John Vassall had his homosexuality: Harry Houghton had his drink. To get more drink he needed more money. The Russians bided their time.

Houghton's original story, given at his trial, was that his first meeting with Lonsdale happened when he heard a knock on his door one weekend and a smiling man introduced himself as Commander Alexander Johnson. He said that he worked at the naval attaché's office in the American embassy in London and that he had been given Houghton's name by a mutual friend who had known him in Warsaw.

The story seemed to tie up and the visitor was convincing about names and places.

According to his own story, Houghton was led to believe that 'Johnson' was merely checking up on the work being done at Portland because the United States was supplying a great deal of the research data. This sounds a trifle naïve, to say the least, but the money was good (by fifties' standards: it wouldn't go far today) and that was all that mattered to Houghton. Presumably he was able to get Miss Gee to help him because she was in love with him.

As well as meeting him at Waterloo, Lonsdale went down to Dorset and they met at several places in and around there, including the Junction Hotel in Dorchester. This was an urgent and important meeting, at which Lonsdale urged Houghton to find out about tests of the new and improved ASDIC which were going to be made at Portland early the following year.

It was Harry Houghton's liberal expenditure on drink that finally led to questions being asked. A naval security man told a detective that he wasn't too happy about Houghton: he didn't like the 'cut of his jib'. . . . The detective promised to investigate. Houghton and Gee were watched, mainly by the Dorset police, and Houghton's home was searched. What was found was nothing as dramatic as the Ruislip haul, but it did include Admiralty charts, with submarine exercise areas and places used for secret trials clearly marked. There were records of Houghton's secret meetings, test pamphlets concealed in the radiogram, and large amounts of loose cash. In Ethel Gee's handbag they found a questionnaire dealing with twelve aspects of top-secret research on ASDIC.

At the Old Bailey trial, Lonsdale was sent to prison for

twenty-five years, Peter Kroger for twenty, Helen for the same, and Houghton and Gee for fifteen years. Lord Parker, the judge, considered Houghton's conduct 'most culpable of all', for Houghton and to a lesser extent Gee were the only real traitors to Britain.

Only three years into his sentence, Gordon Lonsdale was exchanged for Greville Wynne, and the Krogers for Gerald Brooke, a young London lecturer who was apparently totally innocent of all charges and whose only crime had been to take anti-Communist literature into Russia in his capacity as leader of a party of students.

The case of Gerald Brooke hit the British headlines because his health was damaged during his stay in Lublanka Prison and it was perfectly obvious that on the evidence presented he was innocent of the charge of spying. His case was a perfect example of how the Russians put into practice the Napoleonic idea of bartering an innocent dupe for a valued spy.

It was whispered in certain quarters that there was another spy at the Admiralty, but no one did any serious investigating. The clue, it was said, was provided by a defector. But whatever the truth of that was, in 1962 John Vassall, another Admiralty clerk, was sentenced to eighteen years' imprisonment for espionage.

John Vassall was born in London in 1924 and joined the RAF when the Second World War broke out. He served with the Tactical Air Force in fighters and bombers; when the war ended he wanted a job that would let him travel. The idea of working in an embassy abroad appealed a great deal. Let him tell his own story.

'It all comes back so clearly. I was sitting in the Kremlin-like building which overlooks St James's Park in London when I saw a post in Washington, and another one in Moscow, were vacant. As it happened, the Washington post had just been filled, so with much trepidation I applied for the job in Moscow, being ready for any position that promised a completely new world of excitement and danger.'

How right he would be proved! Perhaps if he had landed the Washington job the whole thing might never have happened. When he got to the Moscow post, he says, ' . . . no words could describe the pleasure and happiness that I felt at having been given this wonderful and exceptional opportunity to travel to what was then a forbidden country about which most people knew very little. It was a unique moment in my life.'

No hint of storm clouds on the horizon.

At first in Moscow he was 'desperately lonely'. It seems that he was being watched through the Russian administration office, this vulnerable and weak young man with his homosexual proclivities. . . .

'In the embassy administration office there were two members of the local staff, one Greek and a younger man named Mikhaelovski [a KGB agent, as he later found out] who had been engaged locally by the embassy staff to interpret and to act as local agent for arranging such matters as helping with the Russian servants, travel facilities, theatre and ballet reservations, shopping expeditions to Moscow and elsewhere.'

Vassall loved going to the theatre, opera, ballet and concerts, and was only too glad to take advantage of the services of the obliging Mikhaelovski.

Vassall was clerk to the naval attaché and he eventually

found a flat with another employee, a junior attaché working for the Joint Press Reading Service. One day the two young men went to have lunch at a restaurant in the city.

'My companion spoke fluent Russian. A woman and a young man joined us at our table. She was attentive, extremely serious and spoke to my companion most of the time, and I think she must have been more than just a total stranger. "Who is the good-looking young man with you," she asked. I did not take much notice of her or her male friend, and I never gave the meeting a second thought at the time, though this may have been the very first contact between the Russian secret service and myself.'

His job was rather low in the social hierarchy of embassy life, but he was nothing if not a social climber and went out of his way to cultivate as many friendships as he could, particularly amongst the staff of other embassies. His boss the naval attaché, with whom he didn't get on too well, formally rebuked him for 'moving in circles too high for my position or station in the Embassy'.

Poor Vassall! One can imagine what his feelings must have been. He decided to get invitations for as many parties as he possibly could, and to hell with the old stick-in-the-mud and his class-ridden prejudices. Vassall was on the way up.

He did get invitations, but that wasn't until later, when the deadly chink in his armour had been discovered, and at especially arranged parties and meetings he was given the rope with which he would, metaphorically speaking, hang himself.

Homosexuality at that time was not tolerated in the way it is today. John Vassall, and those like him, were practically begging to be blackmailed. A man called Alfred Redl, a colonel in the Austrian army who sold information to the Russians during the First World War, had been in a similar situation. The Russians had discovered his secret and played on it till it destroyed him. When the truth came out, two of his Austrian brother officers called on him and left a revolver. Suicide was the only way out. (John Osborne wrote a splendid and moving play about Redl called *A Patriot for Me.*)

At one of these meetings he attended, Vassall, a lamb for the slaughter, was framed: compromising photographs were taken and found their way into the hands of the KGB.

One evening, what had started out as a harmless social diversion soon turned into something very different. The door opened and mysterious people came in.

'At first I could not think who these people were. They had appeared out of nowhere. It was such an incredible encounter that I did not know how to react. As they spoke I realized that they were important and mysterious beings who belonged to an organization that was secret and deadly serious. They were quiet, considerate and polite. I was asked who I was, and how and why I came to be at this flat. Would I show some kind of identification? I had to tell them that I was from the British embassy in Moscow. [A fact they plainly knew already.] Only one of these secret service or KGB figures talked to me. The other man sat there and said nothing.'

That evening, Vassall was allowed to go. But like the fishermen they were, the KGB played their line.

The photographs which compromised Vassall were shown to him after he had been summoned to a further meeting. It was finally decided that he should meet members of the secret service every three weeks at a preselected spot. 'If for any reason I could not get there I was to make contact the next evening or, if this were impossible, the following two evenings. There was also a special meeting place to be used at the end of the month if I were away from Moscow.'

Even now, if only he hadn't been so timid, he could still have got out of the mess. The British ambassador, Sir William Hayter, wrote in his diary that if Vassall had come to him and told him he was being blackmailed, he could have been sent home at once. 'One or two similar cases occurred during my time,' he wrote, 'and in none of them was there any difficulty about exit visas.'

The truth was that Vassall didn't like Sir William very much and didn't feel that he could confide in him.

Meanwhile the meetings with the KGB went on.

'These meetings lasted two or three hours. The sort of question they would ask was whom I liked and disliked at the embassy. It was impressed upon me that no information of a secret kind was being asked for, only a general picture of who was in the embassy and what I thought of them. Gradually the entire staff were included: no one was left out. Nothing I said was ever written down, so they must have had a recording machine somewhere. My interrogator spoke with an American accent. I mentioned this once and he said that he had learned English from the beginning in this way.'

Gradually the KGB began to place more confidence in Vassall's reliability. And one day, feeling that he needed some time off, they invited him to take an Easter holiday on the Black Sea, which is used by the Russians as a holiday area.

'Who in our embassy or the government,' Vassall marvels, 'or even in the Foreign Office, would have thought that I would be entertained by officials who were unknown to all the highest security services in London and Washington?'

After the holiday the round of meetings continued. And there were other parties to vary the diet. At one party, 'Mrs Barbara Castle, member of a visiting parliamentary group, took me into a corner and asked me about life in Russia and what I thought of it; and then happily joined in the light entertainment and games, one of which was musical chairs.'

But as the summer of 1955 advanced, the Russians were beginning to press for more important information. 'They wanted something in the way of paper or files,' he said, 'in return for the kindness they had shown towards me.' The Black Sea? One of the party never spoke in English. Vassall, who knew little Russian, says that he was typical of the type portrayed in spy books and films.

'Never once was I treated roughly or manhandled physically by any of these secret service men'. But . . . 'at a further interrogation, before I collapsed under their endless insistence that I should produce something for them, it was hinted that it might be necessary for me to be placed before the "General". This shook me. Who on earth was he and what did he do? Counter-intelligence agents in England asked me, much later, if it was General Serov, Head of the KGB. It may well have been. His office was in the Lublanka Prison and I am afraid that I did not fancy being taken to the most frightening place in the whole of the Soviet Union.'

So the pace was hotting up. And the nitty-gritty of handing over secrets began.

'Towards the end of my time in Moscow the Russians

turned up a new trump. At one of our last meetings I was introduced to a person I had not seen before. Who was he? He gave his name as Gregory and I was to meet him in London when I got back. My heart sank. I had imagined that on leaving Moscow my troubles would all be over and that I could forget about the whole beastly business.'

But Vassall was not to be let off so lightly. His two-year appointment in Moscow had finished, but the nightmare would go on for him in London. He didn't even get much money out of it.

'From time to time the KGB had pressed money on me. But there was so little one could buy. It was possible to save enough from one's salary to purchase necessities from England, which were sent out in the diplomatic bag. But it was simply not done to offer to pay for drinks. . . . When I met the Russian secret service for the last time in Moscow they had some money for me – it was only a nominal amount for travelling expenses.'

Payments allocated to Harry Houghton showed a slightly different set-up. But then Vassall was a blackmail victim, Houghton wasn't.

The KGB allowed Vassall a short holiday in the United States before he returned to England. He reported back to the Admiralty in London and was given a job in the office of the Director of Naval Intelligence.

'My desk was by the window and I could see into the garden of Number Ten Downing Street, the Foreign Office, and the Horseguards entrance facing St James's Park.

'My work was all connected with highly classified material. Every cupboard was full of top secrets, so hot they could not be sent out of the Naval Intelligence Division at all.'

The meetings with Gregory started almost immediately. Vassall never discovered who Gregory was but once he came face to face with him unexpectedly at Covent Garden during the first season in London of the Bolshoi Ballet (the top Russian ballet company) and this gave him the clue that his contact was attached in some capacity or other to the Soviet embassy, as there was a private reception that night.

At the English meetings Vassall was asked the same sort of questions that he'd had to answer in Moscow; Gregory wanted to know details of office personnel, office routine, how many security checks there were and how often, etc. etc.

Every three weeks Vassall had to report at a particular road in Golders Green at 7.30. 'On several occasions a dark formal car passed me but never stopped. I found out later that this was done to see if I had kept the appointment, and also to check whether I was being followed. . . . '

Vassall became quite fond of Gregory. 'We got to know each other well as time went on and had many interesting conversations. One thing used to shock him, or so he led me to believe, and that was the idea that our activities came under the category of espionage. It was really nothing of the sort. It was information needed to brief a possible future summit conference. There was nothing wrong in what I was doing, working for the cause of peace.'

Later he says, 'I had to start using my camera, and that brought me back to earth with a bump!'

After almost a year with the Naval Intelligence Division, Vassall was transferred to the office of the new Civil Lord of the Admiralty, T. G. D. Galbraith MP, to be his private secretary. This was quite a step up in Vassall's career, but

Gregory was upset — the information he was able to collect from his new appointment didn't impress the Russians very much.

Apparently, too, Vassall was getting careless. 'On one awful occasion when I had to meet Gregory, I had invited my parents to *My Fair Lady* and left the documents in the cloakroom. [This must have been at Drury Lane Theatre.] Fortunately they came to no harm, and I picked them up afterwards and carried them with me when I went to say goodbye to the Galbraiths who were leaving Euston on the night sleeper, for Christmas and the New Year.'

It seems that packages often get left behind in loos.

In 1961, round about the time that the news of the Portland spy ring broke, Vassall had a new contact. Gregory had gone back to Moscow and Nicolai took over.

About the arrest of the Portland spies, Vassall says:

'It was a shattering experience. There was so much publicity given to it that I could not fail to be affected by the impact. I thought, how on earth could the Russian intelligence service not have advance warning of this? That evening I was having dinner out, and I had to be terribly careful not to get involved in any conversation on the matter. Nicolai told me that I was nothing whatever to do with the Portland case and that I was not to worry about it at all. In fact I was to cease operating altogether until further notice.'

But the breaking of the Portland ring signalled a tightening up of security inside the Admiralty. The writing was on the wall for John Vassall, though he didn't know it yet.

Then in 1962 ' . . . I was informed by Nicolai that I could start bringing them material again, as the All Clear had gone out from Moscow. I was asked to purchase another camera, but I said this would draw attention to myself.

'I was told to meet Nicolai down on the Embankment near Dolphin Square. There was something odd about this meeting. I had to walk past two telephone boxes, come back, and make a call in the one Nicolai had left. He was to leave a parcel containing a camera and rolls of film in the booth. At the same time that I went into one box a man went into the other and pretended to make a call – I think he must have been watching us all the time. I made a call, picked up the parcel and walked away as quickly as possible. I was nervous, though I couldn't feel anyone watching me. Perhaps by that time they had all the information they wanted.'

It all reads like a bad spy film, and you can't help the feeling that it was some sort of elaborate charade. Perhaps by that time Nicolai had got wind that Vassall's cover was blown. Some men came round to his flat, ostensibly to check the kitchen plumbing. Their story was that someone in the flat above had spilt acid down the sink. But Vassall is convinced that it was an excuse either to search or bug his flat, and that British intelligence were watching him after a tip-off.

He began noticing strange cars following him and was beset by forebodings of disaster. They were proved accurate. One day, leaving the Admiralty, he went to cross the Mall and two men in mackintoshes came forward in real Bond style, flashed warrants and asked Vassall to accompany them to a car waiting beside the statue of Captain Cook.

Now the interrogations began in earnest. The whole case at this time was hidden from the media in a veil of secrecy. Harold Macmillan, the Prime Minister, was forced into setting up the Radcliffe Tribunal to look into the background of the case.

John Vassall served ten years of his eighteen-year sentence and was released in 1972.

He was a weak man, easily led, without the courage to face up to his blackmailers. He certainly had no belief in communism and wasn't really politically minded at all. As he said in his book, 'I have no sympathy with totalitarian regimes. I am perhaps somewhere in the extreme centre.'

He is now a devout Roman Catholic and bitterly regrets his past mistakes.

8
Spies in the Foreign Office

Despite the continued vigilance in Britain maintained by MI5, and in the United States by the FBI, most spies are caught in the West through the first-hand evidence of defectors. Behind the Iron Curtain, in contrast, an army of Soviet police agents are employed to spy on anyone whether they are under suspicion or not. It's known to the West, for instance, that quite often secret police agents select an individual at random and start to investigate his or her activities just as though they were known to be a spy. In other words an individual is guilty until proved innocent; in the West a suspected spy, like a suspect in other branches of crime, is innocent until proved guilty.

We would find this kind of infringement on the individual's right to privacy quite intolerable. . . .

When the public first heard in the press on 7 June 1951 that two top Foreign Office diplomats, Guy Burgess and Donald Maclean, had run away they weren't to guess what would be revealed about spies in top places and how the names of Harold 'Kim' Philby and Anthony Blunt would also come to the fore – with the probability of further revelations to come.

The initial evidence came from Russian defectors and it was this evidence that made Maclean, assisted by Burgess, himself plan to defect to the Soviet Union. Evidence against two further Foreign Office moles, Philby and Blunt, caused Philby to follow later and Blunt to make a full confession. Blunt has remained in England, having received a pardon for turning Queen's Evidence, but has had to forfeit a knighthood that was granted to him for his scholarly academic service to the cause of art. He was Master of the Queen's Pictures, and in that capacity has lectured on TV; he is also a world-famous authority on the French artist Poussin.

What seems incredible is that the British intelligence services freely accepted these four men despite the fact that they had all been active Communists at Cambridge. We saw how this happened in the case of Klaus Fuchs. Although known to be a Communist sympathizer, he was allowed to work on highly confidential scientific research. But his qualifications were high; the four men that we are discussing in this chapter actually got into the intelligence services themselves, and into top positions in those services. Their qualifications were in no way exceptional; they just happened to mix in the right circles and know the right people.

Our Prime Minister, Margaret Thatcher, spoke in the House of Commons in a parliamentary debate in 1979, when the House was discussing the case of Anthony Blunt; this is what she said:

To us today it seems extraordinary that a man who had made no secret of his Marxist beliefs could have been accepted for secret work in any part of the public service, let alone the security service. But that is with the benefit of hindsight. Perhaps standards were relaxed because it was a time of considerable expansion and recruitment to deal with the wartime tasks of the service which were directed against Hitler's Germany.

Many books have been written about the Foreign Office 'moles' and what they did, but although every single fact about their lives and diplomatic careers is known, and everybody who ever met them even if only momentarily seems to have jumped into print, what exactly the information was that they gave away, and how important it was, still is not clear. And it probably never will be, to the layman. Despite the library of books available, including one by Philby himself, written from Moscow probably on the instructions of the Kremlin, the full story will probably never now be known. Although journalists like Chapman Pincher claim to know more than most, a great deal of inside information is still jealously guarded and to reveal too much would constitute a breach of security under the Official Secrets Act. This is a bit like locking the stable door . . . . but official faces still have to be saved. And meanwhile the witch-hunt for the 'fifth man' goes on. (Will it stop at five? I doubt it.)

What *is* clear, however, is that as soon as the Americans discovered that so many senior men in British intelligence had been sending so much priceless information to Russia both during the Second World War and afterwards, their faith in Britain's security systems received such a shattering blow that it will take many years before confidence is restored. Don't forget that when the CIA was started, American officials had been guided by British practices. Now after these revelations it looked as if their faith had been misplaced. We had already had Fuchs and the atom spies; that was bad enough, but now it looked as if the very fabric of British security was corrupted.

Well, things weren't as bad as that, of course. But they were bad enough.

In the thirties, there was a great economic slump in this country and many writers and intellectuals felt that the only answer to the problem, and the only way to save Britain, was to look to the Soviet Union, which after the Bolshevik Revolution of 1917 seemed to be coping beautifully, with their classless society. Join the young Communist Party and destroy capitalism, they said – much as some people are saying today. It was a time of youthful idealism; very few English people had seen communism in action at first hand, and the principals and doctrines taught by people like Marx and Lenin seemed a Utopian dream. When Stalin came to power he kept his dreams of territorial expansion to himself at first. Time enough for that when Hitler and his fascists were destroyed. . . .

So most people only saw the sunny side of communism, the noble ideal that all men are created equal. Nobody bothered to read the small print – so ably illustrated by George Orwell in the warnings of *Animal Farm* and *1984* – that goes on to state, ' . . . but some are more equal than others. . . . '

The intellectual climate was right, and what better place to gain recruits than in the great universities of Oxford and Cambridge? (We've already seen that it was from these two centres of learning that personnel were chosen to run the coding department at Bletchley Park that became known as Station X). As the novelist E. M. Forster wrote, 'The Soviet Union seemed to have all the answers, and an active branch of the Communist Party had recently been founded inside the University.'

Trinity College, the largest college in Cambridge with its undergraduate population of nearly a thousand, its scores of professors and dons, and its vast numbers of clubs and societies catering for all kinds of varied interests and activities, seemed an ideal environment for what was called a Communist cell, or group. (We still use the term 'spy cell'.) Many students joined and helped to recruit others. Even the teaching staff came in. Anthony Blunt was a young don, not an undergraduate. Many famous writers and politicians dabbled with communism briefly, but then grew disillusioned and resigned. Others remained loyal card-carrying Party members. Still others resigned after the Second World War, when the 'iron curtain' descended over Europe and they began to see how far the pure idealism of communism had been distorted by its practitioners.

But some remained loyal to their beliefs and just went underground. They subscribed to the theory that infiltration into the very heart of capitalism would be a far more effective way of destroying it than setting up in opposition. Burgess, Maclean, Philby and Blunt were all at Trinity, Cambridge, and all adopted this course of action. They were all to proclaim that they had seen the error of their ways, in public, but in private held to their communist beliefs tenaciously. Dr Alan Nunn May, who became a top physicist and betrayed atom secrets, was also one of the group.

It wasn't long before representatives of the official Communist Party in London were advised by the Kremlin, who kept a keen watch on Communist cells in the West, to go down to Trinity and arrange a lecture for undergraduates and staff. The more promising material could be signed on officially and authorized to recruit new talent.

Among those authorized to recruit were Blunt and Burgess. In fact it was Burgess the undergraduate who recruited Blunt, the graduate.

Ironically Blunt, Burgess and Maclean all indulged in homosexual practices. Yet unlike the case of John Vassall, where as we've seen, his homosexuality led to blackmail and embroilment in espionage, the four became spies through their political beliefs alone, and homosexuality affected their careers not at all - unless it added to the strain under which they lived and contributed to the heavy drinking in which at least three indulged.

Anthony Blunt gave his own accounts of the reasons that caused him to turn to spying:

In the mid thirties it seemed to me and to many of my contemporaries that the Communist Party of Russia constituted the only firm bulwark against Fascism, since the Western democracies were taking an uncertain and compromising attitude towards Germany. I was persuaded by Guy Burgess that I could best serve the cause of anti-Fascism by joining him in his work for the Russians. This was a case of political conscience against loyalty to country. I chose conscience.

In 1940 he was recruited by MI5 while still in his turn recruiting for Soviet intelligence!

In 1979 Sir Michael Havers, the Attorney General, told the House of Commons:

Let me summarise for the House what happened when Professor Blunt was interviewed by the security service at his home on April 23rd, 1964. He was told of the [new] information [against him] and maintained his denial. He was then offered immunity from prosecution, and in silence for a while, got up, looked out of the window, poured himself a drink, and after a few minutes, confessed.

But the evidence which made Philby confess came from two defectors, Mikhail Goulinevski, a Polish information officer who had worked for the KGB, and Anatole Golitzin, a KGB major. Goulinevski's evidence also named Gordon Lonsdale and the Portland spy ring, and he uncovered another Soviet mole in MI6, George Blake.

It was discovered that Blake had given away the names of forty British agents in Russia, as well as the secrets of a tunnel under Berlin which cost millions and millions of dollars. It was used for tapping Red Army telephone lines.

Blake was arrested and sent to Brixton prison for forty-two years. He later escaped; it was thought this was engineered by the Russians. While in Brixton he met John Vassall and the two, Vassall tells us in his book, had many interesting talks together and discussed their experiences.

While every detail is charted about the way Burgess and Maclean got to Russia, not much is known about Philby's escape. He had always had a drink problem, and apparently the arrests of Lonsdale and Blake drove him into frequent bouts of alcoholism as he felt the net closing round him. He had gone to an unimportant post in Lebanon, and in 1963 Nicholas Elliot of MI6 had driven to Beirut to try to get a confession from him and bring him back to England. There still wasn't enough evidence against Philby to warrant an arrest, but it was only a matter of time. Agents were working on it. But Philby made no attempt to clear his name, although he might have been able to do so. The evidence of defectors isn't valid by itself in a court of law. It needs something concrete to back it up. Otherwise, of course, defectors could accuse whom they liked. (As in some cases they have tried to do.) But Philby chose not to fight and instead scuttled off to Moscow.

Guy Burgess died there, lonely and homesick. Donald Maclean, also by this time an alcoholic, lost his wife to Philby. As a Russian defector said:

They became obscure figures. Even the Russians don't trust traitors, even those giving them useful information. They may allocate you a nice apartment, a good pension and all that, but they will follow you, they will follow you till death. You will never be able to speak freely, and if you try to communicate with the West, you will be given a prepared text. Nothing but a prepared text.

It's very difficult if not impossible to say exactly what information was leaked to the Russians by the four spies over the years. Naturally the Foreign Office is still pretty sensitive about discussing it: the topic hardly shows our diplomatic service in the best light, and in any case the day-to-day business of intelligence is largely 'classified', that is, secret.

It was largely a case of the four leaking a steady stream of material over the years, hardly spectacular if taken in isolation, but cumulatively invaluable.

Of the four, Kim Philby was the most successful spy. He worked for the Russians on and off from 1934 to 1963. In 1941 he was in MI6's Iberian section; in 1942 he was put in charge of North Africa and Italy, as well as Spain and Portugal. He says in his autobiography that he always had easy access to any file he wanted to consult. He must have passed to Moscow an incalculable amount of information about most countries in the world which MI6 had on file.

Perhaps 1944 was the year of his greatest triumph. MI6 decided to create a new department to spy on their allies, the Russians, and their Communist satellites. Philby was chosen to set up this section. According to Graham Greene the novelist, who with Malcolm Muggeridge was also in intelligence during the war, Philby made an excellent job of it. One can imagine the importance to the Russians of having the very department organized to spy on them run by one of their own agents; the whole situation out-Bonds Bond by a million miles. . . .

Philby nearly ran into a spot of bother in 1945. An employee of a Russian consulate in Turkey named Volkov asked for political asylum in England, in return for naming some Soviet spies operating in the U K. The old, old story . . . But the difference between this instance and all the others we have mentioned in this book is that the person Volkov was offering to tell the names to was Philby!

Or rather, to qualify this a little, as Philby was considered to be the department's Soviet expert, he was delegated to fly out to Istanbul to collect the defector. Philby was pretty sure that his own name would be on Volkov's list, so it was imperative that Volkov must not be allowed to reach England. If he did, Philby would be unmasked.

He never did reach England. When Philby arrived in Istanbul, he found that the young man had mysteriously vanished, never to be heard of again. At least that was the story Philby told MI6 on his return. (He might later have reflected that it was a pity that he couldn't silence Goulinevski and Golitzin in the same way; though I believe that by that time he was past caring.)

In 1949 Philby was promoted and sent to Washington as first secretary in the British embassy. This was of course a cover, his real post being chief MI6 officer in charge of a large section that collaborated with the C I A and the F B I. It was while he was here that the news came through about the flight of his friends and colleagues Burgess and Maclean. His career received a blow from which it never recovered. The CIA became suspicious of him, he was sent back to London and questioned. But there was no proof against him. Then came the defectors' stories and his flight from Beirut, where he was working as a journalist.

Donald Maclean, the next most important of the four spies, was also at the embassy in Washington, where he was sent in 1944. Before that he had been secretary to the British embassy in Paris, where he had met Belinda, the girl he was later to marry, who would follow him to Russia before she left him for Philby.

While not able to give out hard scientific facts like Fuchs, his political knowledge was every bit as important. He knew the general heads of agreement between Great Britain, Canada and the USA: he knew where they disagreed, where they would cooperate and where they wouldn't. He also knew how many atom bombs Britain had, the amounts of uranium 235 available and how many bombs we had the resources to make. He perhaps knew enough to make understandable the American Foreign Secretary's remark when the news broke, 'My God, he knew everything!'

While in America Maclean was appointed Secretary to the Anglo-American committee on the future use of atomic energy; while that wasn't very important in itself, it did mean that he had a pass to the Atomic Energy Commission in Washington, where he could help himself to the files. And he did!

Blunt and Burgess were smaller fish. Or so it seems at present. Burgess dabbled on the fringes of the diplomatic service, even joining the BBC as a talks producer (his name can be found in old copies of *Radio Times*!) before his eventual recruitment to the upper echelons of the Foreign Office as personal assistant to Hector McNeil, Minister of State. He had joined as a member of the News Department, but in this post most of the information that came into his hands would have already been published.

His main job as a spy would have been to give background assessments of foreign policy from time to time; and to do what he could to persuade friends and colleagues that Britain's anti-Soviet policy was wrong and misguided and that the Americans were not to be trusted.

Anthony Blunt left MI5 at the end of the Second World War and he didn't involve himself in much espionage after that, as far as is known. His main usefulness to the Russians was the information he was able to slip them about the running and staffing of MI5 itself and later about German intelligence networks. His particular job involved knowing about exiled governments and political parties in London, particularly the National Democrats who were opposed to Nazi Germany, and the Russian anti-communist parties.

An interesting theory about what Blunt and Philby might have done in the Second World War to help Russia was put forward in a BBC talk in 1981.

In 1943 the Soviets set up the National Committee of Free Germany. It consisted of captured German officers and German communists who wanted to sabotage the Nazi Party. Anthony Eden, who at that time was British Foreign Secretary, asked for information on the committee and on whether it would be useful to the Allies.

It was Blunt's job to provide this information. The official attitude of the Foreign Office was that it wasn't worth taking seriously. The Bishop of Chichester had warned Eden that it was a 'communist bid for the control of West Germany after the war'. Eden exploded, calling the bishop a 'pestilent priest' and telling him to mind his own business. William Strang, assistant under-secretary of State, said the bishop was simply 'raising the Communist bogy. He and his like will lead us into a new war in half a generation.'

There were other dissident groups in Germany. A top-secret Foreign Office dossier had said that it would not be to Britain's advantage to link up with them. But at the end of May 1944 the Foreign Office received a memo from the American secret service giving an account of an approach made to them by a man claiming to represent German army commanders who were fed up to the back teeth with the Nazis and were ready to lay down their arms on condition that Russia wasn't allowed to take part in any subsequent peace talks.

The Foreign Office reaction was that this was very 'bogus'.

In the BBC talk, the speaker argued that if Britain had joined up with the National Committee for Free Germany, and thus had been able to undermine Germany from within, it wouldn't have been so easy for the Soviets to divide Germany down the middle after the war and build the Berlin Wall. As it was, of course, the British could never have defeated Germany without the help of the Russian Red Army.

The dissident groups did infiltrate the German army and tried to assassinate Hitler. They had to do this without any outside help, but they were certainly to be taken seriously!

What all this is leading up to is that the report from the Foreign Office that the stories were 'bogus' and that Britain should do nothing to help were written by Blunt! He was aided by Philby, whose job it was to provide information on German affairs for MI6. Britain's lack of direction certainly made it easier for the communists to consolidate their position in Eastern Europe after the war.

All this is speculation, as is so much else in the story of these four men. It's interesting, though, to see from the evidence of a Foreign Office memo how highly thought of in official circles Philby, in particular, was at that time. Frank Roberts, senior official and later ambassador to Moscow and Bonn, wrote a letter to *The Times* in February 1944:

Philby's work is well known to the FO and is of particular interest to us. I'm afraid I must tell you that if we were ever consulted about the possibility of his being released we should be bound to recommend against it because his present work is so important, and he performs it with such exceptional ability.

Mr Roberts was more right than he knew.

The Foreign Office moles fooled an awful lot of people for an awfully long time. And as Tom Lehrer sang in a different context, 'There may be many others but they haven't been discovered.'

New developments in technology will supersede the human spy to a large extent. Spy satellites from the sky can report and convey detailed information in a fraction of the time. There are even anti-satellite satellites, capable of detecting other satellites. Radio ears are forever listening; cameras can operate in unlighted rooms and night-viewing devices let people see in the dark. Heat vibrations can be recorded with such definition that aircraft flying over thick jungle can pinpoint the dying embers of a campfire, or locate a car long after its engine has been switched off.

Like the visual microdot, radio messages can be condensed into a fraction of a second: this is known as burst transmission. Microphones can be aimed to pick up the conversation of two people walking together across an open field more than a hundred yards away.

And so it goes on. Smaller and smaller gadgets abound, many still on the secret list. Others are still on the drawing board.

But machines are not infallible. Human agents are just as essential today as ever they were, if only to collate and classify information or programme a computer. Machines can't decide which information is important, and which can be discarded. It takes man to do that.

Swinburne the poet wrote: 'Glory to Man in the highest, for Man is the master of things.' That dictum is as true now as ever it was. Whether man destroys himself is up to him; but even if he does, it won't be a machine that takes his place.